A LAMAIST VAJRAMAṆḌALA
To be studied in preparation for meditation

[*Frontispiece*

THE SECRET OF
THE GOLDEN FLOWER

A CHINESE BOOK OF LIFE

Translated and explained by
RICHARD WILHELM

with a European Commentary by
C. G. JUNG

With Eleven Plates and Four Text Illustrations

Fourth Impression

NEW YORK
HARCOURT, BRACE & COMPANY
1938

Translated into English by
CARY F. BAYNES

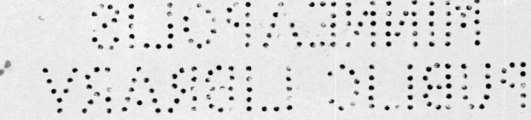

Made and Printed in Great Britain by
PERCY LUND, HUMPHRIES & CO. LTD.
12 Bedford Square, London, W.C.1
and at Bradford

CONTENTS

TEXT AND EXPLANATION BY RICHARD WILHELM

	PAGE
ORIGIN AND CONTENTS OF THE T'AI I CHIN HUA TSUNG CHIH	3
1. Origins of the Book	3
2. The Psychological and Cosmological Premises of the Text	11
TRANSLATION OF THE T'AI I CHIN HUA TSUNG CHIH	21
1. Heavenly Consciousness (the Heart)	23
2. The Primordial Spirit and the Conscious Spirit	26
3. Circulation of the Light and Protection of the Centre	34
4. Circulation of the Light and Making the Breathing Rhythmical	44
5. Mistakes During the Circulation of the Light	50
6. Confirmatory Experiences During the Circulation of the Light	54
7. The Living Manner of the Circulation of the Light	57
8. A Magic Spell for the Far Journey	59
Remarks	71
Summary of the Chinese Concepts on which is based the idea of the *Golden Flower* or *Immortal Body*	73

COMMENTARY BY C. G. JUNG

INTRODUCTION	77
1. Difficulties Encountered by a European in Trying to Understand the East	77
2. Modern Psychology Offers a Possibility of Understanding	83
THE FUNDAMENTAL CONCEPTS	94
1. The Tao	94
2. The Circular Movement and the Centre	96

	PAGE
PHENOMENA OF THE WAY	106
1. The Disintegration of Consciousness	106
2. *Animus* and *Anima*	114
THE DETACHMENT OF THE CONSCIOUSNESS FROM THE OBJECT	121
THE FULFILMENT	128
CONCLUSION	136
EXAMPLES OF EUROPEAN *Maṇḍalas*	137
DESCRIPTION OF THE PLATES	138
APPENDIX: IN MEMORY OF RICHARD WILHELM. By C. G. JUNG	139

TRANSLATOR'S PREFACE

THE original German edition of *The Secret of the Golden Flower*, of which the following is the authorized English translation, appeared first in the autumn of 1929. On March 1st, 1930, Richard Wilhelm died. In May, 1930, memorial services in his honour were held in Münich, and Jung was asked to deliver the principal address. The latter finds an appropriate place in the English version,[1] which is published a year or more after the co-author's death. The address will be welcomed, not only for what it tells the reader of Wilhelm, but for the further light it throws on the standpoint of the East.

The relation of the West to Eastern thought is a highly paradoxical and confusing one. On the one side, as Jung points out, the East creeps in among us by the back door of the unconscious, and strongly influences us in perverted forms, and on the other we repel it with violent prejudice as concerned with a fine-spun metaphysics that is poisonous to the scientific mind.

If anyone is in doubt as to how far the East influences us in secret ways, let him but briefly investigate the fields covered to-day by what is called " occult thought ". Millions of people are included in these movements and Eastern ideas dominate all of them. Since there is nowhere any sign of a psychological understanding of the phenomena on which the ideas are based, they undergo a complete twisting and are a real menace in our world.

A partial realization of what is going on in this direction, together with the Westerner's native ignorance and mistrust of the world of inner experience, build up the prejudice against the reality of Eastern wisdom. When the wisdom of the Chinese is laid before a Westerner, he is very likely to ask with a sceptical lift of the brows why such profound wisdom did not save China from its present horrors. Of course, he does not stop to think that the Chinese asks with an equal scepticism why the much boasted scientific knowledge of the West, not to mention its equally boasted Christian ethics, did not save it from a World War. But as a matter of fact, present conditions in China do not invalidate Chinese wisdom, nor does the Great War prove the futility of science. In both cases we are dealing with the negative sides of the principles under which East and West live, and it has not yet been given, either to individuals or to nations, to manage the

[1] See Appendix, p. 139.

vices of their virtues. Mastery of the inner world, with a relative contempt for the outer, must inevitably lead to great catastrophes. Mastery of the outer world, to the exclusion of the inner, delivers us over to the dæmonic forces of the latter and keeps us barbaric despite all outward forms of culture. The solution cannot be found either in deriding Eastern spirituality as impotent, or by mistrusting science as a destroyer of humanity. We have to see that the spirit must lean on science as its guide in the world of reality, and that science must turn to the spirit for the meaning of life.

This is the point of view established in *The Secret of the Golden Flower*. Through the combined efforts of Wilhelm and Jung we have for the first time a way of understanding and appreciating Eastern wisdom which satisfies all sides of our minds. It has been taken out of metaphysics and placed in psychological experience. We approach it with an entirely new tool, and are protected from the perversions the East undergoes at the hands of the cult-mongers of the West. At the same time, its meaning for us is greatly deepened when we know that, despite the gulf separating us from the East, we follow exactly similar paths when once we give heed to the inner world.

But this book not only gives us a new approach to the East, it also strengthens the point of view evolving in the West with respect to the psyche. The reshaping of values in progress to-day forces the modern man out of a nursery-world of collective traditions into an adult's world of individual choice. He knows that his choice and his fate now turn upon his understanding of himself. Much has been taught him in recent years about the hitherto unsuspected elements in his psyche, but the emphasis is all too often on the static side alone, so that he finds himself possessed of little more than an inventory of contents, the nature of which serves to burden him with a sense of weariness rather than to spur him on to master the problems that confront him. Yet it is precisely the need of understanding himself in terms of change and renewal which most grips the imagination of modern man. Having seen the world of matter disappear before his scientific eye and reappear as a world of energy, he comes to ask himself a bold question; does he not contain within his psyche a store of unexplored forces, which, if rightly understood, would give him a new vision of himself and help safeguard the future for him? In this book his question is answered from two widely different sources, an ancient Chinese yoga system and analytical psychology. Stripped of its archaic setting, *The Secret of the Golden Flower* is the secret of the powers of growth latent in the psyche, and these same powers as they reveal themselves in the minds of Western men also form the theme of Jung's commentary.

In the commentary he has shown the profound psychological development resulting from the right relationship to the forces within the psyche.

*   *   *   *

In the German edition Jung's commentary comes first, followed by Wilhelm's exposition of the text, and then by the text itself. At the author's request, the order has been changed so that his commentary follows the text.

The Chinese words in this edition are in the Anglicized form. For making the necessary transcriptions, I am indebted to Mr. Arthur Waley, and to Colonel Egerton of Kegan Paul, Trench, Trubner and Co. The latter has been kind enough to give his personal attention to the editing of my manuscript.

As a possible aid in keeping in mind the relationships between the various Chinese concepts such as *hsing-ming*, *kuei-shên*, etc., I have added two summaries, one written and one diagrammatic.

Fortunately for me, I have made this translation under the supervision of Dr. Jung, and to that fact, and to the further aid I have received from Mrs. Jung, I owe any success I may have had in meeting the difficulties presented.

It has also been my privilege to have the completed manuscript read and criticized by Dr. Erla Rodakiewicz, and for her invaluable assistance I am deeply grateful.

CARY F. BAYNES.

ZÜRICH,
   March, 1931.

TEXT AND EXPLANATION

BY

RICHARD WILHELM

ORIGIN AND CONTENTS OF THE T'AI I CHIN HUA TSUNG CHIH

1. Origins of the Book

The book comes from an esoteric circle in China. For a long time it was transmitted orally, and then in writing; the first printing is from the *Ch'ien-Lung* period (eighteenth century). Finally, a thousand copies of it were reprinted in Peking in 1920, together with the *Hui Ming Ching*, and were divided among a small group of people who, in the opinion of the editor, understood the questions discussed. In this way I was able to get a copy. The new printing and circulation of the little book was due to a new religious movement growing out of the exigencies of the political and economic conditions in China. There have been formed a series of secret sects whose effort it is to achieve by the practice of secret traditions from ancient times a state of soul lifting them above all the misery of life. The methods used are magical writing, prayer, sacrifice, etc., and, in addition to these, widely prevalent mediumistic *séances*, by means of which direct connection with the gods and the dead is sought. Experiments are also made with the planchette,[1] the flying spirit pencil as the Chinese call it.

But side by side with these practices, there exists an esoteric movement which has devoted itself with energy to the psychological method, that is meditation,

[1] It is a curious fact that the man who circulated this text had written for him by the planchette a preface by Lü Tzŭ, an adept of the T'ang dynasty, to whom these teachings are accredited. This preface certainly deviates very widely from the thoughts given in the book; it is flat and colourless, like the majority of such productions.

yoga practice. The followers of this method, in contradistinction to the European " yogis " to whom these Eastern practices are only a form of sport, achieve almost without exception the central experience. Thus it can be said that, as far as the Chinese mentality is concerned, a completely assured method of attaining definite psychic experiences is commanded. (It must be noted that, as C. G. Jung very correctly points out, Chinese mentality, at least up to very recent times, has been essentially different in some fundamental respects from that of Europeans.) Besides the release from the fetters of an illusory outer world, there are many other goals striven for by the different sects. Those on the highest level use this release by meditation, for the purpose of seeking the Buddhist Nirvana, or, as for example in the present book, they teach that by the union of the spiritual principle in men to the correlated psychogenetic forces one can prepare for the possibility of life after death, not only as a shadow-being doomed to decay, but as a conscious spirit. In addition, and often in connection with this idea, there are schools of thought which try by means of this meditation to exert a psychic influence on certain vegetative animal processes. (As Europeans we would speak here of the endocrine gland-system.) This influence is intended to strengthen, rejuvenate, and normalize the life-processes, so that even death will be overcome in such a way that it fits in as a harmonious ending of life. The spiritual principle, now fitted for an independent continuation of life in the spirit-body, created out of its own forces, deserts the earthly body, which remains behind as a drying shell like that abandoned by a cicada.

The lower strata of these sects sought in this way to acquire magic powers, the ability to banish evil spirits and disease, and here talismans, word and written charms play their part. Sometimes this sort of thing results in mass-psychoses which then find expression in religious or political unrest, as, for example, the Boxer movement. Recently, the unmistakable syncretist tendency of Taoism is shown in the fact that within its institutions members of all of the five world-religions (Confucianism, Taoism, Buddhism, Mohammedanism, and Christianity— even Judaism comes in occasionally for special mention) are included without having to break away from their respective religious communities.

Having thus briefly described the background out of which such movements have grown up in our time, a word must be said as to the sources from which the teachings of the book in question arise. Very remarkable discoveries come to light, and we find that these precepts are much older than their written form. The *T'ai I Chin Hua Tsung Chih* [1] can be traced back to the seventeenth century as having been printed on wooden tablets. The author describes having found an incomplete copy dating from that time in the Liu Li Ch'ang, the old street of dealers in books and antiquities in Peking, and tells how he filled it out later from a friend's book. But the oral tradition goes back even further than that, to the religion of the Golden Elixir of Life (*Chin Tan Chiao*), which developed in the T'ang period in the eighth century. The founder is said to have been the well-known Taoist adept, Lü Yen (Lü Tung-pin), counted later by folk-lore as one of the eight immortals, about whom in the course of time a rich store of myths has gathered. This sect, like all religions, native and foreign, met with tolerance and encouragement in the T'ang period and greatly

---

[1] *The Secret of the Golden Flower* (*T'ai I Chin Hua Tsung Chih*), whose title was changed to *Ch'ang Shêng Shu* (*The Art of Prolonging Human Life*), by the Chinese publisher of this edition.

increased in numbers, but, as it was always an esoteric and secret religion, in the course of time it began to suffer persecution because of members being suspected of political intrigues. Again and again, its adherents were persecuted by a hostile government, lastly in an extremely cruel way by the Manchus, just before their own fall.[1] Many members have turned to the Christian religion, and all, even if they have not actually entered the church, are friendly toward it.

Our book gives the best available account of the religion of the *Golden Elixir of Life* (*Chin Tan Chiao*). The sayings are attributed to Lü Yen, whose other name was Lü Tung-pin, or Lü, the Guest of the Cavern. He lived at the end of the eighth, and at the beginning of the ninth century, and was born in the year A.D. 755. To his sayings a later commentary has been added, but it springs from the same tradition.

Whence did Lü get his esoteric, secret lore? He himself attributes its origin to Kuan Yin-hsi, the Master Yin-hsi of the Pass (Kuan, i.e. Han Ku Pass), for whom, according to tradition, Lao Tzŭ wrote down his *Tao Tê Ching*. As a matter of fact, there are to be found in the system a great many thoughts taken from the esoteric, veiled, mystical teaching in the *Tao Tê Ching*. If we compare, for example, the "gods in the valley" with the "valley-spirit" of Lao Tzŭ, the two are found to be identical. But while Taoism degenerated more and more in the Han period in an external wizardry, due to the fact that the Taoist court magicians were seeking to find by alchemy the philosopher's stone which would create gold out of the baser metals and lend men physical immortality, Lü Yen's movement represented a reform. The alchemistic signs became symbols of psychological

[1] In the year 1891, 15,000 members were killed by Manchu hirelings.

processes. In this respect, there was a close approach to the original ideas of Lao Tzŭ. The latter, however, was altogether a free-thinker, and his follower, Chuang Tzŭ, scorned all the hocus-pocus of yoga practice, nature-healers, and seekers after the elixir of life, although he himself, of course, practised meditation and attained by means of it that view of unity upon which he founded his later, intellectually developed system. In Lü Yen, however, there was a certain faith, a religious trend, which, stimulated by Buddhism, convinced him of the illusory quality of all external things, but in a way clearly different from Buddhism. He seeks, with all his might, the fixed pole in the whirl of phenomena, where the adept can attain eternal life, a thought absolutely foreign to Buddhism, which denies every substantial ego.

Nevertheless, the influence of Mahāyāna Buddhism, which at that time dominated thought in China, is not to be underrated. Buddhist sutras are cited time and again. In our text, indeed, this influence is even greater than can be assumed to have been the case in the *Chin Tan Chiao* in general. In the second half of the third section, explicit reference is made to the method known as "fixating contemplation" (*Chih Kuan*), and the latter is a purely Buddhist method which was practised in the T'ien T'ai School of Chih K'ai.

From this point on, there is to be observed a certain break in the sequence of thought in our essay. On the one hand, the cultivation of the "Golden Flower" is further described, but, on the other hand, there appear purely Buddhist ideas which repudiate the world and emphatically push the goal towards Nirvana. Then follow several sections [1] which have scarcely more value

---

[1] These sections are omitted from the present translation.—(R. W.)

than gleanings, that is, if one considers the spiritually high level and strict sequence of the work as a whole. Moreover, the work towards an inner rebirth by means of contact with the circulation of the Light, and the creation of the divine seed-kernel, is only described in its first stages, although the later stages are named as the goal. (Compare the *Hsü Ming Fang* of Liu Hua Hang where these later stages are more carefully explained.) Therefore, we cannot escape the suspicion that a portion of the manuscript has actually been lost, and substitutions made from other sources. If that is so, it would explain the afore-mentioned break in continuity and the fall in level of the parts not translated.

An unprejudiced reading will bring to notice the fact that these two sources, Taoism and Buddhism, do not suffice to cover the whole range of thought: the form of Confucianism which is based on the *I Ching* is also introduced. The eight fundamental signs (*Pa Kua*) of the *I Ching* are brought into various passages of our text as symbols for certain inner processes, and further on we will try to explain the influence exerted by the application of the symbols. For the rest, since Confucianism has a broad common base with Taoism, the union of these two sets of ideas does not cause a loss in coherence.

Perhaps it will strike many a European reader as remarkable that there appear in the text sayings familiar to him from Christian teaching, while, on the other hand, these same well-known things which in Europe are very often taken only as ecclesiastical metaphors, are here given quite a different perspective because of the psychological connections in which they are placed. We find intuitions and concepts like the following, to select only a few that are especially striking: Light is the life of man. The eye is the light of the body. Man is spiritually reborn out of water and fire, to which must be added " thought-earth " (spirit), as womb, or tilled field. Let us compare the sayings of John : I baptize you with water : after me shall come one who will baptize with the Holy Ghost and with fire ; or : Except a man be born of water and of the spirit, he cannot enter into the kingdom of God. How plastic becomes the thought of " water " as the seed-substance in our text, and how clear the difference between the outward streaming activity which exhausts itself in creation (what is born of flesh remains flesh), and the " backward flowing " movement (*metanoia*) !

The bath, too, plays its part in this rebirth just as it does in the baptism preached by John and in the Christian baptism as well. Even the mystical marriage, which plays such an important rôle in Christian parables, appears several times ; there is also mentioned the child, the boy within ourselves, as well as the bride. (The boy is the *puer aeternus*, the Christ who must be born in us and who, taken another way, is the bridegroom of the soul.) And what is most striking of all, perhaps, even an apparently minor detail, the need of having oil in the lamps so that they can burn brightly, takes on a new and weighty psychological meaning, thanks to our text. It is worth mentioning that the expression Golden Flower (*Chin Hua*), in an esoteric connection, includes the word " light " If one writes the two characters one above the other, so that they touch, the lower part of the upper character and the upper part of the lower character, make the character for " light " (*kuang*). Apparently this secret sign was invented in a time of persecution, when a veil of deep secrecy was necessary to the further promulgation of the doctrine. That was also the reason the teaching always remained limited to secret circles. Even to-day its membership is greater than appears from the outside.

If we ask whither this light-religion points, we can first of all consider Persia, for even in the T'ang period there were Persian temples in many places in China. But if certain points correspond with the religion of Zarathustra, and especially with Persian mysticism, there are, on the other hand, very strong divergences. Another view to be considered is that of a direct Christian influence. In the T'ang period, the religion of the Uigurs, who were connected with the Emperor, was the Nestorian branch of Christianity and stood in high favour, as is witnessed by the well-known Nestorian monument in Sianfu. It was erected in 781, and has both a Chinese and a Syrian inscription. Thus connections between the Nestorians and the *Chin Tan Chiao* are quite possible. Th. Richard went so far as to consider the *Chin Tan Chiao* simply a survival of the old Nestorians. He was led to this view by certain agreements in ritual and certain traditions of the *Chin Tan Chiao* membership which approach closely to the Christian practice. Lately P. Y. Saeki [1] has taken up the theory again, and, supported by the Nestorian liturgy found in Tun-huang by Pelliot, has established a series of further parallels. He even goes so far as to identify Lü Yen, the founder of the *Chin Tan Chiao*, with Adam, the Chronicler of the text of the Nestorian monument, who signs himself with the Chinese name Lü Hsiu-yen. According to this hypothesis, Lü Yen, the founder of the *Chin Tan Chiao*, would have been a Christian of the Nestorian confession! Saeki goes decidedly too far in his delight in identifications: his proofs are all of them almost convincing, but there is always lacking the crucial point which would clinch

[1] *The Nestorian Monument in China.* London, 2nd edition, 1928.

the matter. Many partial proofs do not make a whole one, but we must agree with him at least to the extent of admitting that in the *Chin Tan Chiao* there has been a strong admixture of Nestorian ideas which are also evident in the present manuscript. These ideas seem, on the one hand, very odd in their strange dress, while on the other hand they take on a remarkable " new " sort of life. Here we reach one of those points which prove over and over again:

" East and West are no longer to remain apart."

2. THE PSYCHOLOGICAL AND COSMOLOGICAL PREMISES OF THE TEXT

In the interpretation of the following translation, it is of value to say a few more words about the foundations of the *Weltanschauung* on which the method depends. This philosophy is, to a certain extent, the common property of all Chinese trends of thought. It is built on the premise that cosmos and man in the last analysis obey common laws; that man is a cosmos in miniature and is not divided from the great cosmos by any fixed limits. The same laws rule for the one as for the other, and from the one a way leads into the other. The psyche and the cosmos are related to each other like the inner and outer worlds. Therefore man participates by nature in all cosmic events, and is inwardly as well as outwardly interwoven with them.

Tao, then, the meaning of the world, the way, dominates man just as it does invisible and visible nature (Heaven and Earth). The character for *Tao* in its original form,[1] consists of a head, which must be interpreted as "beginning"; and, under that, the character for "standing still"; which, in the later way of writing, has been omitted. The original meaning, then, is that of a "track which, though fixed itself, leads from the beginning directly to the goal". The fundamenal idea is the idea that *Tao*, though itself motionless, is the means of all movement and gives it law. Heavenly paths are those along which the stars move; the path of man is the way along which he must travel. Lao Tzŭ has used this word in the metaphysical sense, as the final world principle, the "Meaning" existing before there is any realization and not yet divided by the pulling asunder of polar opposites on which all realization depends. This terminology is presupposed in the present book.

In Confucianism there is a certain difference in the terminology. The word *Tao* has here an inner-world significance and means the "right way"; on the one hand, the way of Heaven, on the other, the way of man. To Confucianism, the final principle of an undivided *One* is the *T'ai Chi* (the great ridge-beam, the great pole). The term "pole" occasionally comes in our text also, and is there identical with *Tao*.

Out of *Tao*, that is to say, out of the *T'ai Chi*, there develop the principles of reality; the one pole being light (*yang*) and the other darkness (*yin*). Among European investigators, some have turned first to sexual references for an explanation, but the characters refer to phenomena in nature. *Yin* is shadow, therefore the north side of a mountain and the south side of a river (because during the day the position of the sun makes the river appear dark from the south). *Yang*, in its original form shows

[1] Compare *Ku Chou Pien*, vol. 66, p. 25 ff., which was also consulted as to the analysis of the other characters.

12

flying pennants, and, corresponding to the character *yin*, is the south side of a mountain and the north side of a river. Starting with the meaning of " light " and " dark ", the principle was then expanded to all polar opposites, including the sexual. However, both *yin* and *yang* are only active in the realm of phenomena, and have their common origin in an undivided unity, *yang* as the active principle appearing to condition, and *yin* as the passive principle seeming to be derived or conditioned. It is therefore quite clear that a metaphysical dualism is not at the bottom of these ideas. Less abstract than *yin* and *yang* are the concepts of the creative and the receptive (*Ch'ien* and *K'un*) that originate in the *Book of Changes* [*I Ching*], and are symbolized by Heaven and Earth. Through the union of Heaven and Earth, and through the activity of the two primordial forces within this scene (an activity governed by the one primal law *Tao*), there develop the " ten thousand things ", that is, the outer world.

Viewed objectively as a physical organism, which in all its parts is also a small universe (*Hsiao T'ien Ti*), man is one of the " ten thousand things ". So, according to the Confucians, the inner nature of man comes from Heaven, or, as the Taoists express it, it is a phenomenal form of *Tao*. In his phenomenal form man develops into a multiplicity of individuals in each of whom the central monad is enclosed as the life-principle; but immediately, before birth even, at the moment of conception, it separates into the bi-polar phenomena of essence and life (*hsing* and *ming*). The character for essence (*hsing*) is made up of those for heart (*hsin*), and origin, being born (*shêng*). The heart (*hsin*), according to the Chinese idea, is the seat of emotional consciousness, which is awakened through feeling reactions to impressions received from the external world by the five senses.

That which remains as a substratum when no feelings are being expressed, but which lingers, so to speak, in a transcendental, superconscious, condition, is essence (*hsing*). Varying according to the more exact definition of this concept, essence is either originally good, if looked at from the standpoint of the eternal idea,[1] or it is originally evil, or at least neutral (if taken from the standpoint of empirical evolution),[2] and has to be made into something good by a long development of custom.

Essence (*hsing*), undoubtedly related to *logos*, appears closely knit with life (*ming*) when entering phenomena. The character *ming* really signifies a royal command then, destiny, fate, the fate allotted to a man, so too, the duration of life, the measure of vitality at one's disposal, and thus it comes about that *ming* (life) is closely related to *eros*. Both principles are, so to speak, super-individual. Man as a spiritual being is made human by essence (*hsing*). The individual man possesses it, but it extends far beyond the limits of the individual. Life (*ming*) is also super-individual in that man must simply accept a destiny which does not come from his conscious will. Confucianism sees in it a Heaven-made law to which man must adapt; Taoism takes it as the multi-coloured play of nature which cannot evade the laws of *Tao*, but which, as such, is pure chance; Chinese Buddhism sees it as the working out of *karma* within the world of illusion.

To these dualities there correspond in the corporeal-personal man the following bi-polar tensions. The body is activated by the interplay of two psychic structures: first, *hun*, which I have translated as *animus*,[3] the

[1] See Mencius.
[2] See Hsün K'uang.
[3] Wilhelm's use of the term *animus* lends the latter a meaning quite different from that given it by Jung's concept, where the *animus* is an element in a woman's mind. Jung finds *hun* close to the meaning of *logos*, but the latter term could not be used for *hun*, first, because of there being another Chinese concept still closer

masculine soul, because it belongs to the *yang* principle, and secondly, *p'o*, which belongs to the *yin* principle, and is rendered by me as *anima*.[1] Both are ideas coming from an observation of the events connected with death, and therefore both contain in their written form the sign for daemon, that is, the departed one (*kuei*). The *anima* was thought of as especially linked with the bodily processes; at death it sinks to the earth and decays. The *animus*, on the other hand, is the higher soul; after death it rises in the air, where at first it is active for a time and then evaporates in ethereal space, or flows back into the reservoir of life. In living men, the two correspond in a certain degree to the cerebral and sympathetic nervous system. The *animus* dwells in the eyes, the *anima* in the abdomen. The *animus* is bright and active, the *anima* is dark and earth-bound. The sign for *hun* (*animus*) is made up of the character for "daemon" and "cloud", while that for *p'o* (*anima*) is composed of the characters for "daemon" and "white". This would indicate ideas similar to what we find appearing elsewhere as shadow-soul and body-soul, and without a doubt the Chinese concept is meant to include something like this. None the less, we must be cautious in the matter of derivations, because the most ancient script known in China had no sign for daemon, and so we may perhaps be dealing with primordial symbols whose derivations

to *logos*, i.e. *hsing* (essence), and also because *hun* is described as being a personal factor, while *logos* is strictly impersonal. The expression "spirit soul" as opposed to "earthly soul" would seem to cover the meaning of *hun* as explained by Wilhelm, and in order to avoid a possible confusion in terminology it was planned to make this alteration in the English version, the authors having agreed that a change was advisable. But though the proposed substitution would undoubtedly simplify things for the reader and would involve no change in meaning, still it would require the rearrangement of several paragraphs and thus cause too great a divergence between the two editions. For that reason, the change has not been carried out.—(C. F. B.)

[1] It is to be noted that *p'o* corresponds to only one part of the *anima* as conceived by Jung. In the latter's concept, the spiritual side of the *anima* is quite as important as the animal side.—(C. F. B.)

are lost. In any case, *animus* (*hun*) is the light, *yang*-soul, while *anima* (*p'o*) is the dark, *yin*-soul.

The usual, unchecked,[1] that is, downward movement of the life-processes, is the one in which the two souls are related as the intellectual and animal factors. As a rule, it will be the *anima*, the blind will, which, goaded by passions, forces the *animus* or intellect into its service. At least the *anima* will do this to the extent that the intellect directs itself outward, whereby the powers both of *animus* and *anima* leak away and life consumes itself. A positive result is the creation of new beings in which life continues, while the original being " externalizes itself " and " ultimately is made by things into a thing ". The end result is death. The *anima* sinks, the *animus* rises, and the ego, robbed of its strength, is left behind in a dubious condition.

If the ego has acquiesced in the " externalization ", it follows the downward pull, and sinks into the dull misery of death, only poorly nourished by the illusory images of life which it still attracts to itself without being able to participate in anything actively (hells, hungry souls). But, if the ego has made an effort to strive upward in spite of the process of " externalization ", it maintains for a time (as long, in fact, as it is reinforced by the powers of sacrifice of its survivors) a relatively

[1] The German word used is *rechtläufig*, which means normal flow. In the text it describes forces in the body which flow from up to down, and so in all other instances except the above I have translated it as downward-flowing. When the forces in the body are not allowed to go their natural, downward course, but are dammed up, the movement is described in the text as backward-flowing (*rückläufig*). The yoga system teaches a technique of meditation whereby the natural flow can be thus reversed and the force made to rise to the higher centres, where it is converted into spirit. Leaving out this end result, it is easy for the student of analytical psychology to see a connection between the two streams of force and the concept of extraversion and introversion. An important difference is the fact that extraversion and introversion apply to psychical energy alone, whereas the Chinese concept seems to include both psychical and physiological processes.—(C. F. B.)

happy life, each according to its deserts. In both cases, if the ego follows the *anima*, the personal element retreats and there ensues an involution corresponding to the amount of " externalization ". The being then becomes an impotent phantom because the forces of life fail and its fate is ended. It now partakes of the fruits of its good or bad deeds in heavens or hells, which, however, are not external things, but purely subjective states. The more the being is sunk in these states, the more entangled in them it becomes, till finally it disappears from the plane of existence, of whatever nature that may have been, and then by entering a new womb begins a new existence formed out of its supply of images and memories. This condition is the state of the daemon, the spirit, the departed one, the one who withdraws. The Chinese word for this ghost-being is *kuei*, often wrongly translated by " devil ".

If, on the other hand, it has been possible during life to set going the "backward-flowing", rising movement of the life-forces, if the forces of the *anima* are mastered by the *animus*, then a release from external things takes place. They are recognized but not desired. Thus the illusion is robbed of its strength. An inner, ascending circulation of forces takes place. The ego withdraws from its entanglement in the world, and after death remains alive because " interiorization " has prevented the wasting of the life-forces in the outer world. Instead of these being dissipated, they have made within the inner rotation of monad a centre of life which is independent of bodily existence. Such an ego is a god, *deus, shên*. The character for *shên* means to expand, to produce an effect, in a word, the opposite of *kuei*. In the oldest Chinese script, it is represented by a double serpentine coil, which can also mean thunder, lightning, electrical activity. Such a being survives as long as the inner rotation continues. Also, it can invisibly influence men to great thoughts and noble deeds. The saints and sages of ancient times are beings like these, who for thousands of years have stimulated and educated humanity.

But there remains a limitation. These beings retain a personal character, and are therefore subject to the effects of space and time. Neither are they immortal any more than Heaven and Earth are eternal. Eternal is the Golden Flower only, which grows out of inner liberation from all bondage to things. A man who reaches this stage transposes his ego; he is no longer limited to the monad, but penetrates the magic circle of the polar duality of all phenomena and returns to the undivided *One*, *Tao*. Herein lies a difference between Buddhism and Taoism. In Buddhism, this return to Nirvana is connected with a complete annihilation of the ego, which, like the world, is only illusion. If Nirvana may not be explained as death, cessation, still it is something transcendent. In Taoism, on the other hand, the goal is to preserve in a transfigured form, the idea of the person, the " traces " left by experience. That is the Light, which with life returns to itself, symbolized in our text by the Golden Flower.

As a supplement, we must still add a few words about the use of the eight signs of the *Book of Changes* (*I Ching*) in our text. The sign *Chên* ☳, thunder, the arouser, is life which breaks out of the depths of the Earth; it is the beginning of all movement. The sign *Sun* ☴, wind, wood, gentleness, characterizes the streaming of the reality-forces into the form of the idea. Just as wind pervades all places, so the principle for which *Sun* stands is all-penetrating, and breathes " realization ". The sign *Li* ☲, sun, fire, the lucid (the principle of that which adheres to), plays a great rôle in this light religion. It dwells in the eyes, forms the protecting circle, and effects the rebirth. The sign *K'un* ☷, earth, the receptive, is one of the two primordial principles, namely the *yin* principle which is made real in the forces of the Earth. It is the Earth which, as a tilled field, takes up the seed of Heaven and gives it form. The sign *Tui* ☱, lake, mist, serenity, is an end condition on the *yin* side, and therefore belongs to autumn. The sign *Ch'ien* ☰, Heaven, the creative, the strong, is the reality form of the *yang* principle which fertilizes *K'un*, the receptive. The sign *K'an* ☵ water, the abysmal, is the opposite of *Li* ☲, as is shown in its structure. It represents the region of *eros*, while *Li* stands for *logos*. *Li* is the sun, *K'an* the moon. The marriage of *K'an* and *Li* is the secret magical process which produces the child, the new man. The sign *Kên* ☶, mountain, quietness, represents meditation, which, by keeping external things quiescent, quickens the inner world. Therefore *Kên* is the place where death and life meet, where " *Stirb und Werde* " [1] is consummated.

[1] " Die and come to life ! "

TRANSLATION

OF THE

T'AI I CHIN HUA TSUNG CHIH

1. Heavenly Consciousness (The Heart)

Master Lü Tzŭ said: That which exists through itself is called Meaning (*Tao*). Meaning has neither name nor force. It is the one essence, the one primordial spirit. Essence and life cannot be seen. It is contained in the Light of Heaven. The Light of Heaven cannot be seen. It is contained in the two eyes. To-day I will be your guide and will first reveal to you the secret of the Golden Flower of the Great *One*, and, starting from that, I will explain the rest in detail.

The Great *One* is the term given to that which has nothing above it. The secret of the magic of life consists in using action in order to achieve non-action. One must not wish to leave out the steps between and penetrate directly. The maxim handed down to us is to take in hand the work on the essence. In doing this it is important not to follow the wrong road.

The Golden Flower is the Light. What colour has the Light? One uses the Golden Flower as an image. It is the true power of the transcendent Great *One*. The phrase, " The lead of the water-region has but one taste," refers to it.

In the *Book of Changes* it is said [1]: Heaven created water through the *One*. That is the true power of the Great *One*. If a man attains this *One* he becomes alive; if he misses it he dies. But even if a man lives in the power (air, *prana*) he does not see the power (air), just as fishes live in water but do not see the water. A man dies when he has no life-air, just as the fishes are destroyed when deprived of water. Therefore the adepts have taught the people to hold fast to the primal and to guard the *One*; it is the

---
[1] The references on this and the following pages are to remarks on page 71.

circular course of the Light and the protection of the centre. If one guards this true power, one can prolong the span of life, and can then apply the methods of creating an immortal body by " melting and mixing ".

The work on the circulation of the Light depends entirely on the backward-flowing movement, so that the thoughts are gathered together (the place of Heavenly Consciousness, the Heavenly Heart). The Heavenly Heart lies between sun and moon (i.e. the two eyes).

The *Book of the Yellow Castle* says : In the field of the square inch of the house of the square foot, life can be regulated. The house of the square foot is the face. The field of the square inch in the face : what could that be other than the Heavenly Heart ? In the middle of the square inch dwells the splendour. In the purple hall of the city of jade dwells the god of utmost emptiness and life. The Confucians call it the centre of emptiness ; the Buddhists, the terrace of life ; the Taoists, the ancestral land, or the yellow castle, or the dark pass, or the space of former Heaven. The Heavenly Heart is like the dwelling place, the Light is the master.

Therefore when the Light circulates, the powers of the whole body arrange themselves before its throne, just as when a holy king has taken possession of the capital and has laid down the fundamental rules of order, all the states approach with tribute ; or, just as when the master is quiet and calm, men-servants and maids obey his orders of their own accord, and each does his work.

Therefore you only have to make the Light circulate : that is the deepest and most wonderful secret. The Light is easy to move, but difficult to fix. If it is allowed to go long enough in a circle, then it crystallizes itself : that is the natural spirit-body. This crystallized spirit is formed beyond the nine Heavens. It is the condition of which it is said in the Book of the Seal of the Heart: Silently in the morning thou fliest upward.

In carrying out this fundamental truth you need to seek for no other methods, but must only concentrate your thoughts on it. The book *Lêng Yen* (2) says: By collecting the thoughts one can fly and will be born in Heaven. Heaven is not the wide blue sky, but the place where the body is made in the house of the creative. If one keeps this up for a long time, there develops quite naturally in addition to the body, yet another spirit-body.

The Golden Flower is the Elixir of Life (*Chin Tan*, literally, golden ball, golden pill). All changes of spiritual consciousness depend upon the Heart. Here is a secret charm, which, although it works very accurately, is yet so fluent that it needs extreme intelligence and clarity, and complete absorption and calm. People without this highest degree of intelligence and understanding do not find the way to apply the charm; people without this utmost capacity for concentration and calm cannot keep fast hold of it.

This section explains the origin of the Great Meaning of the world (*Tao*). The Heavenly Heart is the germinal root of the Great Meaning. If a man can be absolutely quiet then the Heavenly Heart will manifest itself. When the feeling springs up and flows out in the natural course, the person is created as primordial creature. This creature abides between conception and birth in true space. When the One note of individuation enters into birth, essence and life are divided in two. From this time on, if the utmost peace is not achieved, essence and life never see each other again.

Therefore it is said in the plan of the Great Pole: The Great *One* includes within itself true power (*prana*), seed, spirit, *animus*, and *anima*. If the thoughts are absolutely quiet so that the Heavenly Heart can be seen, the spiritual intelligence reaches the source unaided. This essence lives indeed in true space, but the splendour of the Light dwells in the two eyes. Therefore the Master teaches the circulation of the Light so that the true essence may be reached. The true essence is the primordial spirit. The primordial spirit is precisely essence and life, and if one accepts what is real in it, it is the primordial power. And the Great Meaning is just this thing.

The Master is further concerned that the people should not miss the way that leads from conscious action to unconscious non-action. Therefore he says: The magic of the Elixir of Life makes use of conscious action in order that non-action may be attained. Conscious action consists in setting the Light in circulation by reflection in order to make manifest the setting free of Heaven. If then the true seed is born, and the right method applied in order to melt and mix it, and in that way to create the Elixir of Life, then one goes through the pass. The embryo, which must be developed by the work of warming, nourishing, bathing, and washing, is formed. That crosses over into the realm of unconscious non-action. A whole year of this fire-period is needed before the embryo is born, sheds the membranes, and passes out of the ordinary world into the holy world.

This method is quite simple and easy. But there are so many transforming and changing conditions connected with it that it is said: Not with one leap can a man suddenly get there. Whoever is seeking eternal life must search for the place whence essence and life originally spring.

2. The Primordial Spirit and the Conscious Spirit

Master Lü Tzŭ said: In comparison with Heaven and Earth, man is like a mayfly. But compared to the Great Meaning, Heaven and Earth, too, are like a bubble and a shadow. Only the primordial spirit and the true essence overcome time and space.

The power of the seed, like Heaven and Earth, is subject to mortality, but the primordial spirit is beyond the polar differences. Here is the place whence Heaven and Earth derive their being. When students understand how to grasp the primordial spirit they overcome the polar opposites of Light and Darkness and tarry no longer in the three worlds (3). But only he who has looked on essence in its original manifestation is able to do this.

When men are set free from the womb the primordial spirit dwells in the square inch (between the eyes), but the conscious spirit dwells below in the heart. This lower fleshly heart has the shape of a large peach: it is covered by the wings of the lungs, supported by the liver, and served by the bowels. This heart is dependent on the outside world. If a man does not eat for one day even, it feels extremely uncomfortable. If it hears something terrifying it throbs; if it hears something enraging it stops; if it is faced with death it becomes sad; if it sees something beautiful it is dazzled. But the Heavenly Heart in the head, when would it have been in the least moved? Dost thou ask: Can the Heavenly Heart not be moved? Then I answer: How could the true thought in the square inch be moved? If it really moves, it is not well. For when ordinary men die, then it moves, but that is not good. It is best indeed if the Light has already fortified itself in a spirit-body and its life-force gradually penetrated the instincts and movements. But that is a secret which has not been revealed for thousands of years.

The lower heart moves like a strong, powerful commander who despises the Heavenly ruler because of his weakness, and has seized for himself the leadership of the affairs of state. But when the primordial castle can be fortified and defended, then it is as if a strong and wise ruler sat upon the throne. The two eyes start the Light circulating like two ministers at the right and the left who support the ruler with all their might. When the ruler in the centre is thus in order, all those rebellious heroes will present themselves with lances reversed ready to take orders.

The way to the Elixir of Life recognizes as supreme magic, seed-water, spirit-fire, and thought-earth: these three. What is seed-water? It is the true, one power (*eros*) of former Heaven. Spirit-fire is the Light (*logos*). Thought-earth is the Heavenly Heart of the middle house (intuition). Spirit-fire is used for effecting, thought-earth for substance, and seed-water for the foundation. Ordinary men make their bodies through thoughts. The body is not only the 7 ft. tall outer body. In the body is the *anima*. The *anima*, having produced consciousness, adheres to it. Consciousness depends for its origin on the *anima*. The *anima* is feminine (*yin*), the substance of consciousness. As long as this consciousness is not interrupted, it continues to beget from generation to generation, and the changes of form of the *anima* and the transformations of substance are unceasing.

But, besides this, there is the *animus* in which the spirit shelters. The *animus* lives in the daytime in the eyes; at night it houses in the liver. When living in the eyes, it sees; when housing itself in the liver, it dreams. Dreams are the wanderings of the spirit through all nine Heavens and all the nine Earths. But whoever is dull and moody on waking, and chained to his bodily form, is fettered by the *anima*. Therefore the concentration of the *animus* is effected by the circulation of the Light, and in this way the spirit is protected, the *anima* subjected, and consciousness annulled. The method used by the ancients for escaping from the world consisted in burning out completely the slag of darkness in order to return to

坐禪圖

坐久忽所知忽覺月在地
泠泠天風來翛然到肝肺
俯視一泓水澄湛無物礙
中有纖鱗遊默默自相契

宜於安
文王之難七
孔子之困陳
蔡一間以止

無事此靜坐一日如兩日
若活七十年便是百四十
靜坐少思寡欲實心養氣存神
此是修真要訣學者可以書紳

Meditation, Stage 1: Gathering the Light.

29

the purely creative. This is nothing more than a reduction of the *anima* and a bringing to perfection of the *animus*. And the circulation of the Light is the magical means of limiting the dark powers and gaining mastery of the *anima*. Even if the work is not directed toward bringing back the creative, but confines itself to the magical means of the circulation of the Light, it is just the Light that is creative. By means of its circulation, one returns to the creative. If this method is followed, plenty of seed-water will be present of itself; the spirit-fire will be ignited, and the thought-earth will solidify and crystallize. And thus can the holy fruit mature. The scarabæus rolls his ball and in the ball there develops life as the effect of the undivided effort of his spiritual concentration. If now an embryo can grow in manure, and shed its skin, why should not the dwelling place of our Heavenly Heart also be able to create a body if we concentrate the spirit upon it?

The one effective, true essence (*logos* united with life), when it descends into the house of the creative, divides into *animus* and *anima*. The *animus* is in the Heavenly Heart. It is of the nature of light; it is the power of lightness and purity. It is that which we have received from the great emptiness, that which has form from the very beginning. The *anima* partakes of the nature of darkness. It is the power of the heavy and the turbid; it is bound to the bodily, fleshly heart. The *animus* loves life. The *anima* seeks death. All sensuous pleasures and impulses to anger are effects of the *anima*; it is the conscious spirit which after death is nourished on blood, but which, during life, is in direst need. Darkness returns to darkness and like things attract each other. But the pupil understands how to distil the dark *anima* so that it transforms itself into Light (*yang*) (4).

In this part there is described the rôle played by the primordial spirit and the conscious spirit in the making of the human body. The Master says: The life of man is like that of a mayfly: only the true essence of the primordial spirit can escape the cycle of Heaven and Earth and the fate of the æons. The true essence proceeds from that which has no polarity and receives the primordial force of polarity whereby it takes the true essence of Heaven and Earth into itself and becomes the conscious spirit. As primordial spirit it receives the essence from father and mother. This primordial spirit is without consciousness and knowledge, but is able to regulate the formative processes of the body. The conscious spirit is very apparent and very effective, and can adapt itself unceasingly. It is the ruler of the human heart. As long as it stays in the body it is the *animus*. After its departure from the body it becomes spirit. While the body is entering into existence, the primordial spirit has not yet made an embryo in which it could incorporate itself. Thus it crystallizes itself in free oneness without poles.

At the time of birth the conscious spirit draws in the power of the air and thus becomes the dwelling of the new-born. It lives in the heart. From that time on the heart is master, and the primordial spirit loses its place while the conscious spirit has power.

The primordial spirit loves peace, and the conscious spirit loves movement. In its movement it remains bound to the feelings and desires. Day and night it wastes the primal seed till the force of the primordial spirit is entirely used up. Then the conscious spirit leaves the shell and goes away.

Whoever has done good in the main, has a power of spirit that is pure and clear when death comes. It passes out by the upper openings of mouth and nose. The pure and light air-power rises upward and floats up to Heaven and becomes the five-fold, present shadow-genius, or shadow-spirit. But if, during life, the primordial spirit was used by the conscious spirit for avarice, folly, desire, and lust, and has committed all sorts of sins, then in the moment of death, the power of the spirit is troubled and confused, and the conscious spirit passes, together with the air, through the lower openings to the door of the belly. For if the power of the spirit is turbid and unclean, it crystallizes downward, sinks down to Hell and becomes a demon. Then not only the primordial spirit loses its nature, but the power and wisdom of the true essence is thereby lessened. Therefore the Master says: If it moves itself, that is not good. If one wants to protect the primordial spirit, one must first not fail to subjugate the knowing spirit. The way to subjugate it leads through the circulation of the Light. If one puts the circulation of the Light into practice, one must forget both body and heart. The heart must die, the spirit live. When the spirit lives, the breath will begin to circulate in a wonderful way. This is what the Master called the best (5). Then the spirit must be allowed to dive down into the abdomen (solar-plexus). The power then mixes with the spirit, and the spirit unites with the power and becomes crystallized. This is the method of putting the hand to it.

In time, the primordial spirit transforms itself in the dwelling of life into the true power. At that time, the method of the turning of the millwheel must be applied, in order to distil it so that it becomes the Elixir of Life. That is the method of concentrated work.

When the Life-Elixir pearl is finished, the holy embryo can be formed; then the work must be directed to the warming and nourishing of the spiritual embryo. That is the method of the finishing.

When the power-body of the child is fully formed, the work must be so directed that the embryo is born and returns again to emptiness. That is the method of the releasing of the hand.

From the most ancient times till to-day, this is not empty talk, but the sequence of the Great Meaning in the real method of producing an eternally living and immortal spirit and holy man.

But if the work is so far successful, then all belonging to the dark principle is entirely destroyed, and the body born into pure light. When the conscious spirit has been transformed into the primordial spirit, then only can one say that it has attained an unending capacity for transformation, and departing from the cycle of births, has been brought to the six-fold (6) present, golden spirit. If this method of ennobling is not applied, how will the way of being born and dying be escaped?

3. Circulation of the Light and Protection of the Centre

Master Lü Tzŭ said: Since when has the expression "circulation of the Light" been revealed? It was revealed by the "True Men of the Beginning of Form" (*Kuan Yin Hsi*) (7). When the Light is allowed to move in a circle, all the powers of Heaven and Earth, of the Light and the Dark, are crystallized. That is what is described as seedlike, or purification of the power, or purification of the concept. When one begins to apply this magic, it is as if, in the middle of one's being, there were a non-being. When in the course of time the work is finished, and beyond the body there is another body, it is as if, in the middle of the non-being, there were a being. Only after a completed work of a hundred days will the Light be real, then only will it become spirit-fire. After a hundred days, there develops by itself in the middle of the Light, a point of the true Light-pole (*yang*). Suddenly there develops the seed pearl. It is as if man and woman embraced and a conception took place. Then one must be quite still in order to await it. The circulation of the Light is the epoch of fire.

In the midst of primal becoming, the radiance of the Light (*Yang Kuang*) is the determining thing. In the physical world it is the sun; in man the eye. The emanation and dissemination of spiritual consciousness is chiefly brought about by this power when it is directed outward (flows downward). Therefore the meaning of the Golden Flower depends wholly on the backward-flowing method.

Man's heart stands under the fire sign (8). The flames of the fire press upward. When both eyes are looking at things of the world it is with vision directed outward. Now if one closes the eyes and, reversing the glance, directs it inward and looks at the room of the ancestors, that is the backward-flowing method. The power of the kidneys is under the water sign. When the instincts are stirred, it runs downward, is directed outward, and creates children. If, in the moment of release, it is not allowed to flow outward but is led back by the force of thought so that it penetrates the crucible of the creative and refreshes heart and body and nourishes them, that also is the backward-flowing method. Therefore it is said: The meaning of the Elixir of Life depends entirely on the backward-flowing method.

Circulation of the Light is not only a circulation of the seed-blossom of the one body, but it is, in the first place, a circulation of the true, creative, formative powers. It has to do, not with a momentary fantasy, but with the exhaustion of the circular course (soul-wanderings) of all the æons. Therefore a breath-pause means a year—according to human reckoning—and a hundred years measured by the long night of the Nine Paths (of re-incarnation).

After a man has the one tone of individuation (9) behind him, he will be born outward according to the circumstances, and not until he is old will he turn a single time to the backward-flowing way. The force of the Light exhausts itself and trickles away. That brings the nine-fold darkness (of rebirths) into the world. In the book *Lêng Yen* (10) it is said: By concentrating the thoughts, one can fly; by concentrating the desires, one falls. When a pupil takes little care of his thoughts and much care of his desires, he gets into the path of depravity. Only through contemplation and quietness does true intuition arise: for that, the backward-flowing method is necessary.

In the book of the *Secret Correspondences* (11), it is said: Release is in the eye. In the *Simple Questions of the Yellow Ruler* (12) it is said: The seed-blossom of the human body must be concentrated upward in the empty space. That refers to it. Immortality is contained in this sentence and also the overcoming of the world is contained in it. That is the common goal of all religions.

The Light is not in the body alone, neither is it only outside the body. Mountains and rivers and the great Earth are lit by sun and moon; all that is this Light. Therefore it is not only within the body. Understanding and clarity, knowing and enlightenment, and all motion (of the spirit), are likewise this Light; therefore it is not just something outside the body. The Light-flower of Heaven and Earth fills all thousand spaces. But also the Light-flower of one body passes through Heaven and covers the Earth. Therefore, just as the Light is circulating, so Heaven and Earth, mountains and rivers, are all rotating with it at the same time. To concentrate the seed-flower of the human body above in the eyes, that is the great key of the human body. Children, take heed! If for a day you do not practise meditation, this Light streams out, who knows whither? If you only meditate for a quarter of an hour, you can set ten thousand æons and a thousand births at rest. All methods take their source in quietness. This marvellous magic cannot be fathomed.

But when the work is started, one must press on from the obvious to the profound, from the coarse to the fine. Everything depends on there being no interruption. The beginning and the end of the work must be one. In between there are cooler and warmer moments, that goes without saying. But the goal must be to reach the breadth of Heaven and the depths of the sea, so that all methods seem quite easy and taken for granted. Only then do we have it in hand.

All holy men have bequeathed this to one another: nothing is possible without contemplation (*fan chao*, reflection). When Confucius says: Knowing brings one to the goal; or when Buddha calls it: The view of the Heart; or Lao Tzŭ says: Inward vision, it is all the same.

Anyone can talk about reflection, but he cannot master it if he does not know what the word means. What has to be changed by reflection is the self-conscious heart, which has to direct itself toward that point where the formative spirit is not yet manifest. Within our 6 ft. body, we must strive for the form which existed before the laying down of Heaven and Earth. If to-day people sit and meditate only one or two hours, looking only at their own egos, and call it contemplation, how can anything come of it?

The two founders of Buddhism and Taoism have taught that one should look at the end of one's nose. But they did not mean that one should fasten one's thoughts to the end of the nose. Neither did they mean that, while the eyes were looking at the end of the nose, the thoughts should be concentrated on the yellow middle. Wherever the eye looks, the heart is directed also. How can the glance be directed at the same time upward (yellow middle), and downward (end of the nose), or alternating, so that it is now up, now down? All that means confusing the finger with which one points to the moon with the moon itself.

What is really meant by this? The expression, "end of the nose," is very cleverly chosen. The nose must serve the eyes as a guiding line. If one is not guided by the nose, either one opens wide the eyes and looks into the distance, so that the nose is not seen, or the lids shut too much, so that the eyes close, and again the nose is not seen. But when the eyes are opened too wide, one makes the mistake of directing them outward, whereby one is easily distracted. If they are closed too much, then one makes the mistake of letting them turn inward, whereby one easily sinks into a dreamy reverie. Only when the eyelids are sunk properly halfway, is the end of the nose seen in just the right way. Therefore it is taken as a guiding line. The main thing is to lower the eye-lids in the right way, and then to allow the Light to stream in of itself, without trying to force the Light to stream in by a concentrated effort. Looking at the nose serves only as the beginning of the inner concentration, so that the eyes are brought into the right direction for looking, and then are held to the guiding line: after that, one can let it be. That is the way a mason hangs up a plumb-line. As soon as he has hung it up, he guides his work by it without continually bothering himself to look at the plumb-line.

Fixating contemplation (13) is a Buddhist method which by no means has been handed down as a secret.

One looks with both eyes at the end of the nose, sits upright and in a comfortable position, and holds the heart to the centre in the midst of conditions (on the fixed pole in the flight of phenomena). In Taoism it is called the yellow middle, in Buddhism the centre in the midst of conditions. The two are the same. It does not necessarily mean the middle of the head. It is only a matter of fixing one's thinking on the point which lies exactly between the two eyes. Then all is well. The Light is something extremely mobile. When one fixes the thought on the midpoint between the two eyes, the Light streams in of its own accord. It is not necessary to direct the attention especially to the central castle. In these few words the most important thing is contained.

"The centre in the midst of conditions," is a very fine expression. The centre is omnipresent; everything is contained in it; it is connected with the release of the whole process of creation. The condition is the portal. The condition, that is the fulfilment of this condition, makes the beginning, but it does not bring about the rest with inevitable necessity. The meaning of these two words is very fluid and subtle.

Fixating contemplation is indispensable, it ensures the strengthening of illumination. Only one must not stay sitting rigidly if worldly thoughts come up, but one must examine where the thought is, where it began, and where it fades out. Nothing is gained by pushing reflection farther. One must be content to see where the thought arose, and not seek beyond the point of origin; for to find the heart (consciousness), to get behind consciousness with consciousness—that cannot be done. We want to bring the states of the heart together in rest, that is true contemplation. What contradicts it is false contemplation. This leads to no goal. When the flight of thoughts keeps extending farther, one should stop and begin contemplating. Let one contemplate and then start concentrating again. That is the double method of strengthening the illumination. It means the circular course of the light. The circular course is fixation. The Light is contemplation. Fixation without contemplation is circulation without Light. Contemplation without fixation is Light without circulation! Take note of that!

The general meaning of this section is that the protection of the centre is important for the circular course of the Light. The last section dealt with the theme that the human body is a very valuable possession when the primordial spirit is master. But when it is used by the conscious spirit, the latter brings it about that, day and night, the primordial spirit is scattered and wasted. When it is completely worn out, the body dies. The method is described whereby the conscious spirit can be subjected and the primordial spirit guarded; that is impossible if one does not begin by making the Light circulate. It is like this: if a splendid house is to be built, a fine foundation must first be found. When the foundation is strong, then only can the work proceed and the base of the walls be deeply and solidly grounded, and the posts and walls built up. If a foundation is not laid in this way, how can the house be completed? The way of cultivating life is exactly like that. The circulation of the Light is to be compared with the foundation of the building. When the foundation stands firm, how quickly it can be built upon! To protect the yellow middle with the fire of the spirit, that is the work of building. Therefore the Master makes especially clear the method by which one enters in the cultivation of life, and bids people look with both eyes at the end of the nose, to lower the lids, to look within, sit quietly with upright body, and fix the heart on the centre in the midst of the conditions.

Keeping the thoughts on the space between the two eyes allows the Light to penetrate. Thereupon, the spirit crystallizes and enters the centre in the midst of the conditions. The centre in the midst of the conditions is the lower Elixir-field, the place of power (solar plexus).

The Master hinted at this secretly when he said: At the beginning of the work one must sit in a quiet room, the body like dry wood, the heart like cooled ashes. Let the lids of both eyes be lowered; then look within and purify the heart, cleanse the thoughts, stop pleasures and conserve the seed. One should sit down daily to meditate with legs crossed. Let the light in the eyes be stopped; let the hearing power of the ear be crystallized and the tasting power of the tongue diminished; that is, the tongue should be laid to the roof of the mouth; let the breathing through the nose be made rhythmical and the thoughts fixed on the dark door. If the breathing is not first made rhythmical it is to be feared that there will be difficulty in breathing, because of stoppage. When one closes the eyes, then one should take as a measure a point on the back of the nose which lies not half an inch below the intersection point of the line of sight, where there is a

嬰兒現形圖

此時丹熟更須慈母惜嬰兒

行住坐卧
抱雛守雌
綿綿若存
念茲在茲

氣穴法名無盡藏
歲包於窓窓包窂
我問空中誰氏子
他云是你主人翁

夫蟾蜍之蟲
孕蜣蛉之子
傳其情交葉
精此其氣和
其神隨物大
小俱得其真

潛龍今已化飛龍
變現神通不可窮
一朝跳出珠光外
滾身直到紫微宮

長養聖軀
內外無塵
沐灌根株
神水溶液

他日雲飛方見真人朝上帝

Meditation, Stage 2 : Origin of a new being in the place of power.

little bump on the nose. Then one begins to collect one's thoughts; the ears make the breathing rhythmical; body and heart are comfortable and harmonious. The Light of the eyes must shine quietly, and, for a long time, neither sleepiness nor distraction must set in. The eyes do not look outward, they drop their lids and light up what is within. There is Light in this place. The mouth does not speak nor laugh. One closes the lips and breathes inwardly. Breathing is at this place. The nose smells no odours. Smelling is at this place. The ear does not hear things outside. Hearing is at this place. The whole heart watches over what is within. Its watching is at this place. The thoughts do not stray outward; true thoughts have continuity in themselves. If the thoughts are lasting, the seed is lasting; if the seed lasts, the power lasts; if the power lasts, then will the spirit last also. The spirit is thought; thought is the heart; the heart is the fire; the fire is the Elixir. When one looks at what is within in this way, the wonders of the opening and shutting of the gates of Heaven will be inexhaustible. But the deeper secrets cannot be effected without making the breathing rhythmical.

If the pupil begins and cannot hold his thoughts to the place between the two eyes; if he closes the eyes, but the power of the heart does not enable him to look at the place of power, the cause is most probably the fact that the breathing is too loud and hasty. Other evils arise from this because body and heart are kept busy trying to suppress forcibly the uprush of power and quick breath.

If the thoughts are only held to the two eyes, but the spirit is not crystallized in the solar plexus (the centre in the midst of the conditions), it is as if one had mounted to the hall but had not yet entered the inner chamber. Then the spirit-fire will not develop, the power remains cold, and the true fruit will hardly manifest itself.

Therefore the Master harbours the fear lest, in their efforts, men only fix their thoughts on the place on the nose, but fail to think of fixing their ideas on the place of power; that is why he used the comparison of the mason with the plumb-line. The mason only uses the plumb-line in order to see if his wall is perpendicular or slanting, and for this the string serves as a guiding line. When he has determined the direction, he can begin the work. But then he works on the wall, not on the plumb-line. That is clear. From this it is seen that fixing the thoughts between the eyes means only what the plumb-line does to the mason. The Master refers again and again to this because he fears his meaning might not be understood. And even if the pupils have grasped the way of doing the thing, he fears they might interrupt their work, and so he says several times: " Only after a hundred days of consistent work, only then is the Light real; only then can one begin work with the spirit-fire." If one proceeds in a collected fashion, after a hundred days there develops spontaneously in the Light, a point of the real creative Light (*yang*). The pupils must examine that with sincere hearts.

4. Circulation of the Light and Making the Breathing Rhythmical

Master Lü Tzŭ said: The decision must be carried out with a whole heart, and, the result not sought for; the result will come of itself. In the first period of release there are chiefly two mistakes:—laziness, and distraction. But that can be remedied; the heart must not enter into the breathing too completely. Breathing comes from the heart (14). What comes out of the heart is breath. When the heart stirs, there develops breath-power. Breath-power is originally transformed activity of the heart. When our hearts go very fast they imperceptibly pass into fantasies which are always accompanied by the drawing of a breath, because this inner and outer breathing hangs together like tone and echo. Daily we draw innumerable breaths and have an equal number of fantasy-representations. And thus the clarity of the spirit is depleted just as wood dries out and ashes die.

Should a man have no images in his mind? One cannot be without images. Should one not breathe? One cannot do without breathing. The best way is to make a cure out of the illness. Since heart and breath are mutually dependent, the circulation of the Light must be united with the rhythm of breathing. For this, Light of the ear is above all necessary. There is a Light of the eye and a Light of the ear. The Light of the eye is the united Light of the sun and moon outside. The Light of the ear is the united seed of sun and moon within. The seed is also the Light in crystallized form. Both have the same origin and are different only in name. Therefore, understanding (ear) and clarity (eye) are one and the same effective Light.

In sitting down, after dropping the lids, one establishes a plumb-line with the eyes and shifts the Light downward. But if the transposition downward is not successful, then the heart is directed toward listening to the breathing. One should not be able to hear with the ear the outgoing and intaking of the breath. What one hears is that it has no tone. As soon as it has tone, the breathing is rough and superficial, and does not penetrate into what is fine. Then the heart must be made quite light and insignificant. The more it is released, the less important it becomes; the less important, the quieter. All at once it becomes so quiet that it stops. Then the true breathing is manifested and the form of the heart can be made conscious. When the heart is light, the breathing is light, for every movement of the heart brings about breathing power. If the breathing is light, the heart is light, for every movement of the breath affects the heart. In order to steady the heart, one begins by cultivating the breathing power. The heart cannot be influenced directly. Therefore the breathing power is used as a handle, and this is what is called protecting the collected breathing power.

Children, do you not understand the nature of motion? Motion can be produced by outside means.

It is only another name for mastery. One can make the heart move merely by running. Should one not be able to bring it to rest then by concentrated quietness ? The great Holy Ones who knew how the heart and breathing power mutually influence one another, have thought out an easier procedure as a way of helping posterity.

In the *Book of the Elixir* (15) it is said: The hen can hatch her eggs because her heart is always listening. That is an important magic spell. The reason the hen can hatch the eggs is because of the power to heat. But the power of the heat can only warm the shells; it cannot penetrate into the interior. Therefore with her heart she conducts this power inward. This she does with her hearing. In this way she concentrates her whole heart. When the heart penetrates, the power penetrates, and the chick receives the power of the heat and begins to live. Therefore a hen, even when she has left her eggs, always has the attitude of listening with bent ear. Thus the concentration of the spirit is not interrupted. Because the concentration of the spirit suffers no interruption, neither does the power of heat suffer interruption day or night, and the spirit awakes to life. The awakening of the spirit is accomplished because the heart has first died. When a man can let his heart die, then the primordial spirit wakes to life. To kill the heart does not mean to let it dry and wither away, but it means that it is undivided and gathered into one.

Buddha said: When you fix your heart on one point, then nothing is impossible for you. The heart easily runs away, so it is necessary to gather it together by means of breathing power. Breathing power easily becomes coarse, therefore it has to be refined by the heart. When that is done, can it then happen that it is not fixed ?

The two mistakes of laziness and distraction must

be combated by quiet work that is carried on daily without interruption; then results will certainly be achieved. If one is not seated during meditation, one will often be distracted without noticing it. To become conscious of the inattention is the mechanism by which to do away with inattention. Laziness of which a man is conscious, and laziness of which he is unconscious, are a thousand miles apart. Unconscious laziness is real laziness; conscious laziness is not complete laziness, because there is still some clarity in it. Distraction comes from letting the spirit wander about; laziness comes from the spirit not yet being pure. Distraction is much easier to correct than laziness. It is as in sickness: if one feels pains and itchings, one can help them with remedies, but laziness is like a disease that is attended by loss of feeling. Distraction can be overcome, confusion can be straightened out, but laziness and absent-mindedness are heavy and dark. Distraction and confusion at least have a place, but in laziness and absent-mindedness the *anima* alone is active. In inattention the *animus* is still present, but in laziness pure darkness rules. If one becomes sleepy during meditation, that is an effect of laziness. Breathing alone serves to remove laziness. Although the breath that flows in and out through the nose is not the true breath, the flowing in and out of the true breath is connected with it.

While sitting, one must, therefore, always keep the heart quiet and the power concentrated. How can the heart be made quiet? By breathing. The heart alone must be conscious of the flowing in and out of the breath; it must not be heard with the ears. If it is not heard, then the breathing is light; if light, it is pure. If it can be heard, then the breathing power is heavy; if heavy, then it is troubled; if it is troubled, then laziness and absent-mindedness develop and one wants to sleep. That is self-evident.

How to use the heart correctly during breathing must be understood. It is use without use. One need only let the Light fall quite gently on the hearing. This sentence contains a secret meaning. What does it mean to let the Light fall? It is the radiance of the Light of one's own eyes. The eye looks inward only and not outward. To sense brightness without looking outward means to look inward; it has nothing to do with an actual looking within. What does hearing mean? It is hearing the Light of one's own ear. The ear listens only within and does not listen to what is outside. To sense brightness without listening to what is outside, is to listen to what is within; it has nothing to do with actually listening to what is within. In this sort of hearing, one only hears that there is no sound; in this kind of seeing, one only sees that no shape is there. If the eye is not looking outward and the ear is not harkening outward, they close themselves and are inclined to sink inward. Only when one looks and harkens inward does the organ not go outward nor sink inward. In this way laziness and absent-mindedness are done away with. That is the union of the seed and the Light of the sun and moon.

If, as a result of laziness, one becomes sleepy, one should stand up and walk about. When the spirit has become clear one can sit down again. If there is time in the morning, one may sit during the burning of an incense candle, that is the best. In the afternoon, human affairs interfere and one can therefore easily fall into laziness. It is not necessary to have an incense candle. But one must lay aside all complications and sit quite still for a time. In the course of time there will be success without one's getting lazy and falling asleep.

The chief thought of this part is that the most important thing about the circulation of the Light is making the breathing rhythmical. The further the work advances, the deeper becomes the teaching. The pupil must bring heart and breathing into relationship during the circulation of the Light in order to avoid the burden of laziness and distraction. The Master fears lest, during the *séance*, when the beginners have lowered their lids, confused fantasies may arise, because of which, the heart will begin to beat so that it is difficult to guide. Therefore he teaches the work of counting the breath and fixing the thoughts of the heart in order to prevent the power of the spirit from flowing outward.

Because breath comes out of the heart, unrhythmical breathing comes from the heart's unrest. Therefore one must breathe in and out quite softly so that it remains inaudible to the ear, and only the heart quietly counts the breaths. When the heart forgets the number of breaths, that is a sign that the heart has gone off into the outer world. Then one must hold the heart steadfast. If the ear does not listen attentively, or the eyes do not look at the back of the nose, it often happens that the heart runs off outside, or that sleep comes. That is a sign that the condition is going over into confusion and absent-mindedness, and the seed-spirit must be brought into order again. If, in lowering the lids and taking direction from the nose, the mouth is not tightly closed and the teeth are not clenched firmly together, it can easily happen that the heart hastens outward; then one must close the mouth quickly and clench the teeth together. The five senses order themselves according to the heart, and the spirit must call the breathing-power to aid, in order that heart and breath are harmonized. In this way there is need at most of daily work of a few quarter-hours for heart and breathing to come of themselves into the right sort of collaboration and harmony. Then one need no longer count and breathing becomes rhythmical of its own accord. When the breathing is rhythmical the mistakes of laziness and distraction disappear of their own accord.

5. Mistakes During the Circulation of the Light

Master Lü Tzŭ said : Your work will gradually draw itself together and mature, but before you reach the condition in which you sit like a withered tree before a cliff, there are many other possibilities of error which I would like to bring to your special attention. These conditions are only recognized when they have been personally experienced. I will enumerate them here. My school differs from the Buddhist yoga school (*Chao Tsung*) (16), in that it has confirmatory signs for each step of the way. First I would like to speak of the mistakes and then of the confirmatory signs.

When one sets out to carry out one's decision, care must be taken to see that everything can proceed in a comfortable, easy manner. Too much must not be demanded of the heart. One must be careful that, quite automatically, heart and power correspond to one another. Only then can a state of quietness be attained. During this quiet state the right conditions and the right place must be provided. One must not sit down (to meditate) in the midst of frivolous affairs. That is to say, one must not have any vacuities in the mind. All entanglements must be put aside and one must be supreme and independent. Nor must the thoughts be directed toward the right procedure. If too much trouble is taken there is danger of doing this. I do not mean that no trouble is to be taken, but the right behaviour lies in the middle way between being and non-being. If one can attain purposelessness through purpose, then the thing has been grasped. Supreme and without confusion, one goes along in an independent way. Furthermore, one must not fall victim to the ensnaring world. The ensnaring world is where the five kinds of dark demons disport themselves.

端拱寅心圖

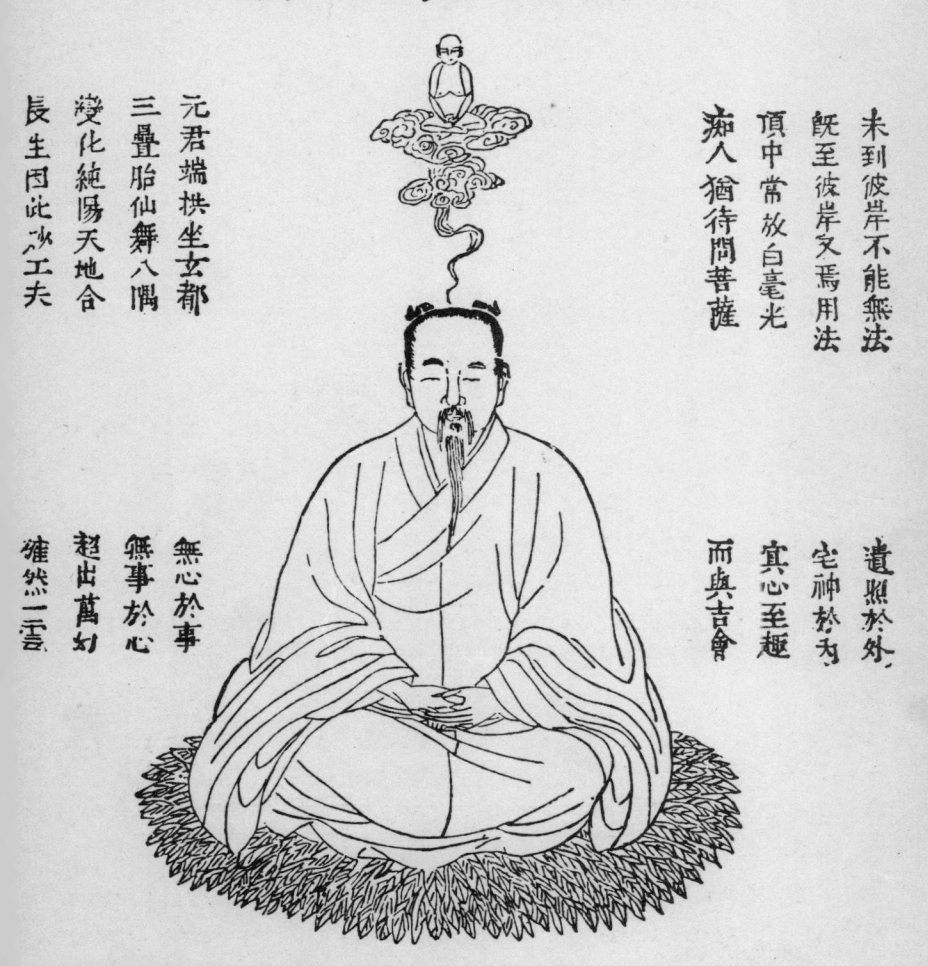

元君端拱坐玄都
三疊胎仙舞八隅
變化純陽天地合
長生因此次工夫

無心於事
無事於心
超出萬幻
雖然一云

未到彼岸不能無法
既至彼岸又焉用法
頂中常放白毫光
癡人猶待問菩薩

遣照於外
宅神於內
寅心至趣
而與吉會

Meditation, Stage 3: Separation of the spirit-body for independent existence.

51

This is the case, for example, when, after fixation, one has chiefly thoughts of dry wood and dead ashes, and few thoughts of the resplendent spring on the great earth. In this way one sinks into the world of darkness. The power is cold there, breathing is heavy, and many images of coldness and decay display themselves. If one tarries there long one enters the world of plants and stones.

Nor must a man be led astray by the ten thousand ensnarements. This happens if, after the quiet state has begun, one after another all sorts of ties suddenly appear. One wants to break through them and cannot; one follows them, and feels relieved by this. This means the master has become a servant. If a man tarries in this state long he enters the world of illusory desires.

At best, one goes to Heaven; at the worst, one goes among the fox-spirits (17). Such a fox-spirit might also occupy himself in the famous mountains enjoying the wind and the moon, the flowers and fruits, and taking his pleasure in coral trees and jewelled grass. But after he has been occupied thus for three to five hundred years, or at the most, for a couple of thousand years, his reward is over and he is born again into the world of turmoil.

All of these are wrong paths. When a man knows the wrong paths, he can then inquire into the confirmatory signs.

The meaning of this section (18) is to call attention to the wrong paths of meditation so that one can enter the place of power instead of the cave of fantasy. This is the world of demons. This, for example, is the case if one sits down to meditate, and sees light flames or bright colours appear, or if one sees Bodhisatvas and gods approach, or any other similar fantasies. Or, if one is not successful in uniting power and breathing, if the water of the kidneys cannot rise, but presses downward, the primordial power becomes cold and the breathing heavy. Then the gentle light powers of the great Earth are too few, and the empty fantasy-world is entered. Or, when one has sat a long time, ideas rise up in crowds and one tries to stop them, but it cannot be done; one submits to being driven by them and feels easier. When this happens, one must under no circumstances go on with meditation but must get up and walk around a little while until heart and power are again in unison; only then can one return to meditation. In meditating, a man must have a sort of conscious intuition, so that he feels power and breathing unite in the field of the Elixir; he must feel that a warm release belonging to the true Light begins to stir dimly. Then he has found the right place. When this right place has been found, one is released from the danger of getting into the world of illusory desire or dark demons.

6. Confirmatory Experiences during the Circulation of the Light

Master Lü Tzŭ said: There are many kinds of confirmatory experiences. One must not content oneself with small demands but must rise to the thought that all living creatures have to be freed. It is not permissible to be trivial and irresponsible in heart. One must strive to make deeds prove one's words.

If, when there is quiet, the spirit has continuously and uninterruptedly a sense of great gaiety as if intoxicated or freshly bathed, it is a sign that the Light principle in the whole body is harmonious; then the Golden Flower begins to bud. When, furthermore, all openings are quiet, and the silver moon stands in the middle of Heaven, and one has the feeling that the great Earth is a world of light and brilliancy, that is a sign that the body of the heart opens itself to clarity. It is a sign that the Golden Flower is opening.

Furthermore, the whole body feels strong and firm so that it fears neither storm nor frost. Things by which other men are displeased, when I meet them, cannot cloud the brightness of the seed of the spirit. Yellow gold fills the house; the steps are white jade. Rotten and stinking things on Earth that come in contact with one breath of the true power will immediately live again. Red blood becomes milk. The fragile body of the flesh is sheer gold and diamonds. That is a sign that the Golden Flower is crystallized.

The *Book of Successful Contemplation* (*Ying Kuan Ching*) says: The sun sinks in the Great Water and magic pictures of trees in rows arise. The setting of the sun means that in Chaos (in the world before phenomena, that is, the intelligible world), a foundation is laid: that is the condition free of opposites (*wu chi*). Highest good is like water, pure and spotless. It is the ruler of the Great Polarity, the god who is revealed in the sign for that which greatly disturbs, *Chên* (19). *Chên* is also symbolized by wood, wherefore the image of trees in rows appears. A sevenfold row of trees means the light of the seven body-openings (or heart-openings). In the north-west is the direction of the creative. When it moves on one place farther, the abysmal is there. The sun which sinks into the Great Water is the image for the creative and abysmal. The abysmal is the direction of midnight (mouse, *Tzŭ*, north). At the winter solstice the thunder (*Chên*) is in the middle of the Earth quite hidden and covered up. Only when the sign *Chên* is reached, does the Light-pole come over the earth again. That is the picture representing the row of trees. The rest can be correspondingly inferred.

The second part refers to the building of the foundation on this. The great world is like ice, a glassy world of jewels. The brilliancy of the Light is gradually crystallized. That is why a great terrace arises and upon it, in the course of time, Buddha appears. When the Golden Being appears who should it be but Buddha? For Buddha is the Golden Saint of the Great Enlightenment. This is a great confirmatory experience.

Now there are three confirmatory experiences which can be tested. The first is that, when one has entered the state of meditation, the gods (20) are in the valley. Men are heard talking as though at a distance of several hundred paces, each one quite clear. But the sounds are all like an echo in a valley. One can always hear them, but never oneself. This is called the presence of the gods in the valley.

At times the following can be experienced: as soon as one is quiet, the Light of the eyes begins to blaze up, so that everything before one becomes quite bright as if one were in a cloud. If one opens one's eyes and seeks the body, it is not to be found any more. This is called: In the empty chamber it grows light. Inside and outside, everything is equally light. That is a very favourable sign. Or, when one sits in meditation, the fleshly body becomes quite shining like silk or jade. It seems difficult to remain sitting; one feels as if drawn upward. This is called: The spirit returns and pushes against Heaven. In time, one can experience it in such a way that one really floats upward.

And now it is possible to leave all three of these experiences. But not everything can be expressed. Different things appear to each person according to his gifts. If one experiences these things, it is a sign of a good aptitude. With these things it is just as it is when one drinks water. One can tell for oneself whether the water is warm or cold. In the same way a man must convince himself about these experiences, then only are they real.

7. The Living Manner of the Circulation of the Light

Master Lü Tzŭ said : When there is gradual success in producing the circulation of the Light, a man must not give up his ordinary occupation in doing it. The ancients said : When occupations come to us, we must accept them ; when things come to us, we must understand them from the ground up. If the occupations are regulated by correct thoughts, the Light is not scattered by outside things, but circulates according to its own law. Even the still-invisible circulation of the Light gets started this way, how much more then is it the case with the true circulation of the Light which has already manifested itself clearly. When in ordinary life one has the ability always to react to things by reflexes only, without any admixture of a thought of others or of oneself, that is a circulation of the Light arising out of circumstances. It is the first secret.

If, early in the morning, a man can rid himself of all entanglements and meditate from one to two double hours, and then can orientate himself toward all activities and outside things in a purely objective, reflex way, and if this can be continued without any interruption, then after two or three months, all the perfected Ones come from Heaven and sanctify such behaviour.

The preceding section deals with the blissful fields that are entered when one succeeds in the work. The aim of this part is to show the pupils how they must shape their work more finely day by day so that they can hope for an early attainment of the Elixir of Life. How does it happen that the Master just here speaks of the fact that a man ought not to give up his calling in life as a citizen ? It might be thought from this that the Master wanted to prevent the pupil from attaining the Elixir of Life quickly. He who knows replies to this : Not at all ! The Master is concerned lest the pupil may not have fulfilled his *karma*, therefore he speaks in this way. Now if the work has led into the blissful fields, the heart is like the reflecting surface of water. When things come, it mirrors things; when they go, spirit and power spontaneously unite and do not allow themselves to be carried away by outside things. That is what the Master means when he says: Every interference of the thought with other people and with oneself must be completely given up. When the pupil succeeds in concentrating with true thoughts on the place of power, he does not have to start the Light circulating, and the Light circulates by itself. But when the Light circulates, the Elixir is made spontaneously, and the performance of worldly tasks at the same time is not a hindrance. It is different at the beginning of the work of meditation when spirit and power are still scattered and confused. If worldly affairs cannot then be kept at a distance, and a quiet place found where one can concentrate with all one's power, and thus avoid all disturbances from ordinary occupations, then one is perhaps industrious in the morning and certainly lazy in the evening. How long would it take in this way till a man attained to the real secrets? Therefore it is said: When one begins to apply the work, one should put aside household affairs. And, if that is not wholly possible, someone ought to be engaged to look after them, so that one can take pains with complete attention. But when the work is so far advanced that secret confirmations are experienced, it does not matter if, at the same time, the ordinary affairs are put in order, so that one can fulfil one's *karma*. This means the living manner of the circulation of the Light. Long ago, the true man of the purple Polar-Light (Tzŭ-yang Chên Jên), made a saying: When a man lives in contact with the world, and yet still in harmony with the Light, then the round is round and the angular has angles; then he lives among men concealed, yet visible, different, and yet the same, and none can compass it; then no one takes note of our secret life and being. The living manner of the circulation of the Light has just this meaning: To live in contact with the world and yet in harmony with the Light.

8. A Magic Spell for the Far Journey

Master Lü Tzŭ said: Yü Ch'ing has left behind him a magic spell for the Far Journey:

" Four words crystallize the spirit in the place of power.
In the sixth month the white snow is suddenly seen to fly.
At the third watch the disk of the sun sends out shining rays.
On the water blows the wind of gentleness.
Wandering in Heaven, one eats the spirit-power of the receptive.
And the deeper secret within the secret:
The land that is nowhere, that is the true home . . . . "

These verses are full of mystery. The meaning is: The most important thing in the Great Meaning is the four words: non-action in action. Non-action prevents a man from becoming entangled in form and image (substantiality). Action in non-action prevents a man from sinking into numbing emptiness and a dead nothingness. The effect depends entirely on the central *One*; the freeing of the effect is in the two eyes. The two eyes are like the pole of the Great Wain which turns the whole of creation; they cause the poles of Light and Darkness to rotate. The Elixir depends from beginning to end on the *One*; the metal in the middle of the water, that is, the lead in the water-region. Heretofore we have spoken of the circulation of the Light, indicating thereby the initial release which works from without upon what lies within. This is to aid one in obtaining the Master. It is for the pupils in the beginning stages. They go through the two lower transitions in order to gain the upper one. After the sequence of events is clear and the nature of the release is known, Heaven no longer withholds the Meaning, but reveals the ultimate truth. Disciples! keep it secret and hold to it strictly!

The circulation of the Light is the inclusive term.

The further the work advances, the more can the Golden Flower bloom. But there is a still more marvellous kind of circulation. Till now we have worked from the outside on what is within; now we tarry in the centre and rule what is external. Hitherto, it was a service in aid of the Master; now it is a dissemination of the commands of this Master. The whole relationship is now reversed. If one wants to penetrate the more delicate regions by this method, one must first see to it that body and heart are completely controlled, that one is quite free and at peace, letting go of all entanglements, untroubled by the slightest excitement, with the Heavenly Heart exactly in the middle. Then let one lower the lids of the two eyes as if one received a holy edict, a summons to the minister. Who would dare disobey? Then one illumines the house of the abysmal (water, *K'an*) with both eyes. Wherever the Golden Flower appears, the true Light of polarity goes out to meet it. The principle of that which adheres to (lightness, *Li*), is light outside and dark within; it is the body of the creative. Darkness enters and becomes master. The result is that the heart (consciousness), becomes dependent on things, is directed outward, and is tossed about on the stream. When the rotating Light shines within the heart, it does not become dependent on things, the power of the Dark is limited, and the Golden Flower shines with concentration. It is then the collected Light of polarity. Things which are related attract each other. Thus the polarity Light-line of the abysmal presses upward. It is not only the Light in the abyss, but it is creative Light meeting creative Light. As soon as these two substances meet each other, they unite inseparably, and unceasing life begins; it comes and goes, rises and falls of itself, in the house of the primordial power. One is aware of effulgence and infinity. The whole body feels lighter and would like to fly. This is the state of which it is said: Clouds fill the thousand mountains. Gradually it [life] goes here and there quite quietly; it rises and falls imperceptibly. The pulse stands still and breathing stops. This is the moment of true creative unity, the state of which it is said: The moon gathers up the ten thousand waters. In the midst of this darkness, the Heavenly Heart suddenly begins a movement. This is the return of the one Light, the time when the child comes to life.

But the details of this must be carefully explained. When a person looks at something, listens to something, eyes and ears move and follow the things until they have passed. These movements are all underlings, and when the Heavenly ruler follows them in their tasks, it means: To live together with demons.

If now, during every movement and every moment of rest, a person lives together with people and not with demons, then the Heavenly ruler is the true man. When he moves and we move with him, the movement is the root of Heaven. When he is quiet and we are quiet with him, this quietness is the cave of the moon. When he continues to alternate movement and quietness, one ought to go on with him unceasingly in movement and quietness. If he rises and falls with inhaling and exhaling, we must rise and fall with him. That is what is called going to and fro between the root of Heaven and the cave of the moon.

When the Heavenly Heart still preserves calm, movement before the right time is a fault of softness. When the Heavenly Heart has already moved, the movement that follows afterwards, corresponding with it, is a fault of rigidity. As soon as the Heavenly Heart is stirring, one must immediately mount with all one's feeling to the house of the creative. Thus the Light of the spirit sees the summit that is the leader. This movement is in accord with the time. The Heavenly Heart rises to the summit of the creative, where it expands in complete freedom. Then suddenly it wants the deepest silence, and one must lead it speedily and with one's whole being into the yellow castle. Thus the eyes behold the central yellow dwelling place of the spirit.

When the desire for silence comes, not a single thought arises; he who is looking inward suddenly forgets that he looks. At this time, body and heart must be left completely free. All entanglements disappear without trace. Then I no longer know at what place the house of my spirit and my crucible are. If a man wants to make certain of his body, he cannot get at it. This condition is the penetration of Heaven into Earth, the time when all wonders return to their roots.

The *One* is the circulation of the Light. If one begins, it is at first scattered and one tries to collect it; the six senses are not active. This is the care and nourishment of one's own origin, the filling up of the oil when one goes to receive life. When one is far enough to have gathered it, one feels light and free and need take no further trouble. This is the quieting of the spirit in the space of the ancestors, the taking possession of former Heaven.

When one is so far advanced that every shadow and every echo has disappeared, so that one is quite quiet and firm, it is safe within the cave of power, where all that is miraculous returns to its roots. The place is not changed but divides itself. It is incorporeal space where a thousand and ten thousand places are one place. The time is not changed, but divides itself. It is immeasurable time when all the æons are like a moment.

Meditation, Stage 4 : The centre in the midst of the conditions.

As long as the heart has not attained complete peace, it cannot move itself. One moves the movement and forgets the movement; this is not movement in itself. Therefore it is said: If, when stimulated by external things, one is moved, it is the instinct of the being. If, when not stimulated by external things, one is moved, it is the movement of Heaven. The being that is placed over against Heaven, can fall and come under the domination of the instincts. The instincts are based upon the fact that there are external things. They are thoughts that go on beyond their own position. Then movement leads to movement. But, when no idea arises, the right ideas come. That is the true idea. If things are quiet and one is quite firm, the release of Heaven suddenly moves. Is this not a movement without purpose? Action in inaction has the same meaning.

As to the beginning of the poem, the two first lines refer entirely to the activity of the Golden Flower. The two next lines are concerned with the mutual interpenetration of sun and moon. The sixth month is the adhering (*Li*) fire. The white snow that flies, is the true darkness of polarity in the middle of the fire sign, that is about to turn into the receptive. The third watch is the abysmal (*K'an*) water. The sun's disk is the one polar line in the sign for water, which is about to turn into the creative. In this is contained the way to take the sign for the abysmal and the way to reverse the sign for the adhering (fire *Li*). The following two lines have to do with the activity of the pole of the Great Wain, the rise and fall of the whole release of polarity. Water is the sign of the abysmal; the eye is the wind of softness (*Sun*). The light of the eyes illumines the house of the abysmal, and controls there the seed of the great Light. " In Heaven " means the house of the creative (*Ch'ien*).

"Wandering, in Heaven, one eats the spirit-power of the receptive." This shows how the spirit penetrates the power, and how Heaven penetrates the Earth; this happens so that the fire can be nourished.

Finally, the two last lines point to the deepest secret which cannot be dispensed with from the beginning to the end. It is the washing of the heart and the purification of the thoughts; it is the bath. The holy science takes as a beginning the knowledge of where to stop, and as an end, stopping at the highest good. Its beginning is beyond polarity and it empties again beyond polarity.

Buddha speaks of the transient, the creator of consciousness, as being the fundamental truth of religion. And, in our Taoism, the expression "to produce emptiness" contains the whole work of completing life and essence. All three religions agree in the one proposition, the finding of the spiritual Elixir in order to pass from death to life. In what does this spiritual Elixir consist? It means forever tarrying in purposelessness. The deepest secret in our teaching, the secret of the bath, is confined to the work of making the heart empty. Therewith the heart is set at rest. What I have revealed here in a word is the fruit of decades of effort.

If you are not yet clear as to how far all three parts can be present in one part, I will make it clear to you through the threefold Buddhist contemplation about emptiness, delusion, and the centre.

Emptiness comes as the first of the three contemplations. All things are looked upon as empty. Then follows delusion. Although it is known that they are empty, things are not destroyed, but a man attends to his affairs in the midst of the emptiness. But though one does not destroy things, neither does one pay attention to them; this is contemplation of the centre. While practising contemplation of the empty, one also knows that one cannot destroy the ten thousand things, and still one does not notice them. In this way the three contemplations fall together. But, after all, strength is in visioning the empty. Therefore, when one practises contemplation of emptiness, emptiness is certainly empty, but delusion is empty also, and the centre is empty. It needs a great strength to practise contemplation of delusion; then delusion is really delusion, but emptiness is also delusion, and the centre is also delusion. Being on the way of the centre, one also creates images of the emptiness, but they are not called empty, but are called central. One practises also contemplation of delusion, but one does not call it delusion, one calls it central. As to what has to do with the centre, more need not be said.

This section mentions first Yü Ch'ing's magical charm for the Far Journey. The magical charm states that the secret wonder of the Meaning is the developing of something out of nothing. In that spirit and power unite in crystallized form, there appears, in the course of time, in the middle of the emptiness of nothing, a point of the true fire. During this time, the more quiet the spirit becomes, the brighter is the fire. The brilliance of the fire is compared with the sun's heat in the sixth month. Because the blazing fire causes the water of the abysmal to vaporize, the steam is heated, and when it has passed the boiling point, it mounts upward like flying snow. It is meant by this that snow is seen to fly in the sixth month. But because the water is vaporized by the fire, the true power is awakened; yet, when Darkness is at rest, Light begins to move; it is like midnight. Therefore adepts call this time the time of the living midnight. At this time, one works at the power with the purpose of making it rise and flow backward, and fall, flowing downward, like the turning of the wheel of the rising sun. Therefore it is said: At the third watch, the disk of the sun sends out shining rays. The rotation method makes use of breathing to blow on the fire of the gates of life: in this way the true power is successfully brought to its original place. Therefore it is said that the wind blows on the water. Out of the single power of former Heaven, there develops the out- and the in-going breath of later Heaven and its power to set aflame.

The way leads from the sacrum upward in a backward-flowing manner to the summit of the creative, and on through the house of the creative; then it sinks through two stories in a downward-flowing way into the solar plexus, and warms it. Therefore it is said: Wandering in Heaven, one eats the spirit-power of the receptive. Because the true power goes back into the empty place, in time, power and form become rich and full; body and heart become glad and cheerful. If, by the work of the turning of the Wheel of the Doctrine, this cannot be achieved, how otherwise should one be able to enter upon this Far Journey? What it amounts to is this: The crystallized spirit flows back to the spirit-fire, and by means of the greatest quiet, one fans the "fire in the middle of the water", which is in the middle of the cave. Therefore it is said: And the deeper secret within the secret: the Land that is nowhere, that is the true home.

The pupil has penetrated in his work into mysterious territory; but, if he does not know the method of melting, it is to be feared that the Elixir of Life will not be produced. Therefore the Master has revealed the secret strictly guarded by the former holy men. When the pupil keeps the crystallized spirit fixed within the cave of power, and, at the same time, lets greatest quietness hold sway, then out of the obscure darkness, a something develops out of the nothingness, that is, the Golden Flower of the Great *One* appears. At this time the conscious Light is differentiated from the Light of the essence. Therefore it is said: To move when stimulated by external things, leads to its going downward and outward and creating a man. That is conscious Light. If, at the time the true power has been copiously gathered together, the pupil does not let it flow downward and outward, but allows it to flow backward, that is the Light of Life; the method of the turning of the water-wheel must be used. If one continues to turn, the true power returns to the roots, drop by drop. Then the water-wheel stops, the body is clean, the power is fresh. One single turning means one Heavenly cycle, that which Master Chiu has called a small Heavenly cycle. If one does not wait to use the power until it has been collected sufficiently, it is then too tender and weak, and the Elixir is not formed. If the power is there and not used, then it becomes too old and rigid, and also the Elixir of Life will hardly be produced. When it is neither too old nor too tender, then is the right time to use it with intention. This is what Buddha means when he says: The phenomenon flows into emptiness. This is the sublimation of the seed into power. If the pupil does not understand this principle, and lets the power stream away downward, then the power forms into seed; this is what is meant when it is said: Emptiness finally flows into the phenomenon. But every man who unites bodily with a woman feels pleasure first and then bitterness; when the seed has flowed out, the body is tired and the spirit languid. It is quite different when the adept lets spirit and power unite. That brings first purity and then freshness; when the seed is transformed, the body is healthy and free. There is a tradition that the old Master P'êng grew to be 880 years old because he made use of serving maids to nourish his life, but that is a misunderstanding. In reality, he used the method of sublimation of spirit and power. In the Elixirs of Life symbols are generally used, and in them the adhering fire (*Li*) is frequently compared to a bride, and the water of the abyss to the boy (*puer aeternus*). From this arose the misunderstanding about Master P'êng having restored his virility through femininity. These are mistakes that have forced their way in later.

But adepts can only use the means of overthrowing the abysmal and the adhering (*Li*) when their purposes are sincerely in the work, otherwise a pure mixture is not produced. The true purpose is subject to the Earth. The colour of the Earth is yellow; therefore in books on the Life Elixir, it is symbolized by the yellow germ. When the abysmal and the adhering (*Li*) unite, the Golden Flower appears; the golden colour is white, and therefore white snow is used as a symbol. But worldly people who do not understand the secret words of the books of the Life Elixir, have misunderstood yellow and white in that they have taken it as a means of making gold out of stones. Is not that foolish?

An ancient adept said: Formerly, every school knew this jewel, only fools did not know it wholly. If we reflect on this we see that the ancients really attained long life by the help of the seed-power present in their own bodies, and did not lengthen their years by swallowing this or that sort of elixir. But worldly people lose the roots and cling to the tree-tops. The Book of the Elixir also says: When the right man (white magician) makes use of wrong means, the wrong means work in the right way.

By this is meant the transformation of seed into power. "But if the wrong man uses the right means, the right means work in the wrong way." By this is meant the bodily union of man and woman from which spring sons and daughters. The fool wastes the most precious jewel of his body in uncontrolled pleasure, and does not know how to conserve the power of his seed. When it is finished, the body perishes. The Holy and Wise men have no other way of taking care of their lives except by destroying lusts and safeguarding the seed. The seed that is conserved is transformed into power, and the power, when there is enough of it, makes the creatively strong body. The difference shown by ordinary people depends only upon how they apply the downward-flowing way or the backward-flowing way.

The whole meaning of this section is directed toward making clear to the pupil the method of the filling up the oil in meeting life. Here the eyes are the chief thing. The two eyes are the handle of the polar constellation. Just as Heaven turns about the polar star as a centre point, so among men the right intention must be the master. Therefore the completion of the Life Elixir depends entirely on the harmonizing of the right intention. Then, if it is said that the foundation can be laid in a hundred days, first of all the degree of industry in work must be taken into account, and the degree of strength in the physical constitution. Whoever is eager in the work, and has a strong constitution, succeeds more quickly in turning back the water wheel of the river. When a person has found the method of making thoughts and power harmonize with one another, he can complete the Elixir within a hundred days. But whoever is weak and lazy will not produce it even after the hundred days. When the Elixir is completed, spirit and power are pure and clear; the heart is empty, the essence manifest, and the light of consciousness transforms itself into the Light of the essence. If the Light of the essence is held permanently, the abysmal and the adhering (fire Li) have intercourse spontaneously. When the abysmal and the fire mix, the holy fruit is borne. The ripening of the holy fruit is the effect of a great Heavenly cycle. Further elucidation stops with the method of the Heavenly cycle.

This book is concerned with the cultivation of life and shows at first how one takes hold of it by looking at the bridge of one's nose. The method of making firm and letting go is in another book, the *Hsü Ming Fang* (Methods of Prolonging Life).

REMARKS

1. This commentary probably comes from the seventeenth or eighteenth century.
2. *Lêng Yen* is the Buddhist *Lañkavātārasūtra*.
3. Heaven, earth, hell.
4. Light is meant here as a world-principle, the positive pole, not as light that shines.
5. The four stages of re-birth are characterized here. The re-birth (out of water and spirit), is the development of the pneumatic body within the perishable body of the flesh. In this there is shown a relationship to the thoughts of Paul and John.
6. The five-fold present spirit into which the good man is transformed in his dark strivings at his death, is limited to the region of the five senses, and is therefore still imprisoned on this earth. Re-birth effects his transition into the sixth, the spiritual realm.
7. A pupil of Lao Tzŭ.
8. The two psychic poles are here contrasted with one another. They are represented as *logos* (heart, consciousness), to be found under the fire sign, and *eros* (kidneys, sexuality), under the water sign. The "natural" man lets both these forces work outwardly (intellect and the process of procreation), and in this way they "stream out" and are consumed. The adept turns them inward and brings them together, whereby they fertilize one another and thus produce a psychically red-blooded, and therefore strong, life of the spirit.
9. The character "*ho*", translated by "individuation" is written with the symbol for "power", inside an "enclosure". Thus it means the form of the entelechy imprinted in the monad. It is the loosening of a unit of power and the veiling of it with the seed-powers that lead to incarnation. The process is represented as connected with a sound. Empirically it coincides with conception. From that time on, there takes place an ever-advancing "development", "unfolding", until birth brings the individual to light. From then it continues automatically farther till the power is exhausted and death ensues.
10. *Lañkvatārasūtra*, Buddhist *sūtra*.
11. *Yin Fu Ching*, Taoist *sūtra*.
12. *Su Wên*, a Taoist work of a later time which purports to come from the mythical ruler Huang Ti.
13. The method of fixating contemplation (*Chih Kuan*), is

the meditation method of the Buddhist T'ien T'ai school. It alternates between the fixation of the thoughts by breathing practices, and contemplation. In the following, some of its methods are taken over. The "conditions" are the "circumstances", the "environment", which, in conjunction with the "causes" (*yin*), start the rotation of the illusion. In the "centre of the conditions", there is, quite literally, the "fixed pole in the flight of phenomena".

14. The Chinese character for "breath" (*hsi*) is made up of the character *tzŭ* "of", "self", and the character *hsin* "heart", "consciousness". It can also be interpreted as "coming from the heart", but, at the same time, it describes the condition in which "the heart is at one with itself", i.e. quietness.

15. A secret book of the sects of the golden life-pill.

16. In Japanese, *Zen*.

17. According to Chinese folk-lore, foxes can also cultivate the Life-Elixir; they thus attain the capacity of transforming themselves into human beings. They correspond to the nature demons of Western mythology.

18. This section shows plainly a Buddhist influence. The temptation mentioned here consists in one's being impelled by these fantasies to take them as real, and to succumb to them. (Compare the scene where Mephistopheles puts Faust to sleep by means of his demon.)

19. Compare the *I Ching*, section *Shuo Kua* (the Signs). *Chên* is the sign for thunder, spring, east, wood. The creative, Heaven, in this division, is in the north-west. The abysmal is in the north.

Ch'ien, the creative, Heaven.

K'an, the abysmal, water, the moon

Kên, keeping quiet, the mountain, stillness.

Tui, serenity, lake, mist.

Chên, that which greatly disturbs, wood, thunder

K'un, the receptive, earth.

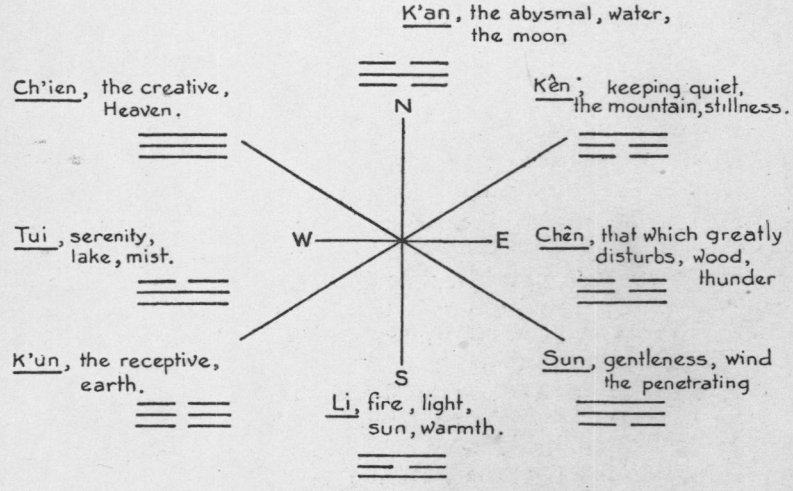

Li, fire, light, sun, warmth.

Sun, gentleness, wind the penetrating

20. Compare Lao Tzŭ, *Tao Tê Ching*, section 6.

Summary [1] *of the Chinese Concepts on which is based the idea of the "Golden Flower" or Immortal "Body".*

Tao the undivided, Great *One*, gives rise to two opposite reality principles, Darkness and Light, *yin* and *yang*. These are at first thought of only as forces of nature apart from man. Later, the sexual polarities and others as well, are derived from them. From *yin* comes *K'un*, the receptive feminine principle; from *yang* comes *Ch'ien*, the creative masculine principle; from *yin* comes *ming*, life; from *yang*, *hsing* or essence.

Each individual contains a central monad which, at the moment of conception, splits into life and essence, *ming* and *hsing*. These two are super-individual principles, and so can be related to *eros* and *logos*.

In the personal bodily existence of the individual they are represented by two other polarities, a *p'o* soul (or *anima*) and a *hun* soul (or *animus*). All during the life of the individual these two are in conflict, each striving for mastery. At death they separate and go different ways. The *anima* sinks to earth as *kuei*, a ghost-being. The *animus* rises and becomes *shên*, a revealing spirit or god. *Shên* may in time return to *Tao*.

If the life-forces flow downward, that is, without let or hindrance into the outer world, the *anima* is victorious over the *animus*; no "spirit body" or "Golden Flower" is developed, and, at death, the ego is lost. If the life-forces are led through the "backward-flowing" process, that is, conserved, and made to "rise" instead of allowed to dissipate, the *animus* has been victorious, and the ego persists after death. It is then possessed of *shên*, the revealing spirit. A man who holds to the way of conservation all through life may reach the stage of the "Golden Flower", which then frees the ego from the conflict of the opposites, and it again becomes part of *Tao*, the undivided, Great *One*.

[1] This summary and the following diagram have been arranged by the English translator.

Diagram of the Chinese Concepts concerned with the development of the "Golden Flower", or Immortal "Spirit Body".

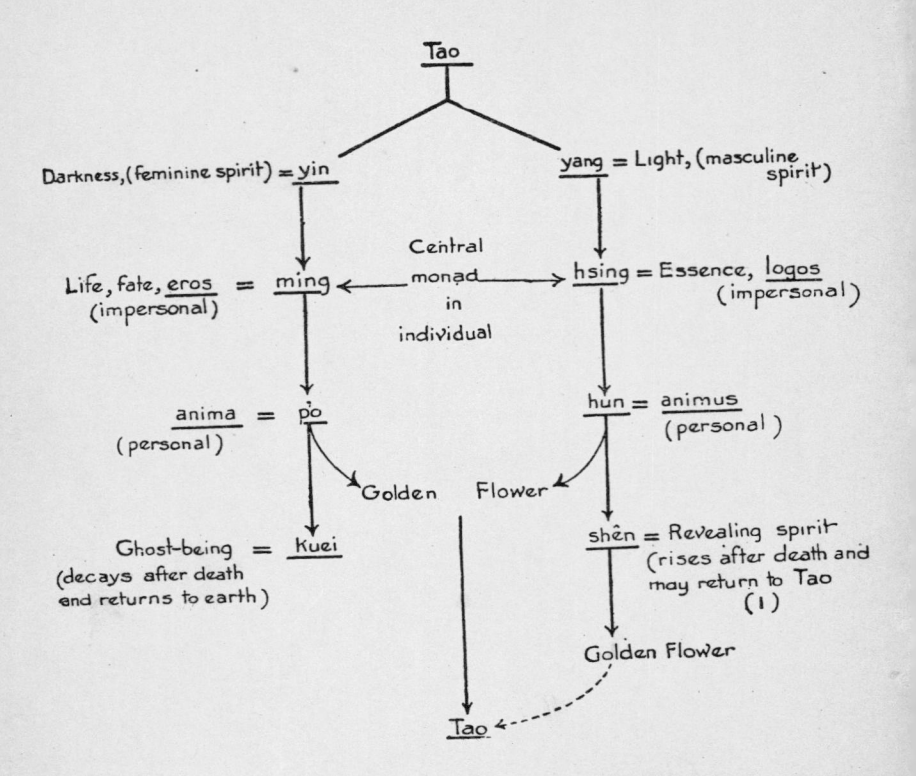

```
                              Tao
                           /       \
                          /         \
Darkness,(feminine spirit) = yin    yang = Light, (masculine spirit)
                   │                   │
                   ▼       Central     ▼
Life, fate, eros  =  ming ←— monad —→ hsing = Essence, logos
   (impersonal)              in            (impersonal)
                         individual
                   │                   │
                   ▼                   ▼
   anima  =  p'o                 hun = animus
  (personal)                          (personal)
                   │                   │
                   ↘  Golden  Flower ↙
                   │                   │
                   ▼                   ▼
  Ghost-being = Kuei              shên = Revealing spirit
 (decays after death                  (rises after death and
  and returns to earth)                may return to Tao
                                              (1)
                          │            │
                          ▼            ▼
                         Tao ←------ Golden Flower
```

[1] As there is ample evidence in the text to show that Buddhist influences represented the Golden Flower as coming ultimately only from the spiritual side, that fact has been indicated by the dotted arrow leading down from *shên*. In undiluted Chinese teaching, however, the creation of the "Golden Flower" depends on the equal interplay of both the *yang* and *yin* forces.

COMMENTARY
BY
C. G. JUNG

INTRODUCTION
    1. Difficulties encountered by a European in trying to understand the East.
    2. Modern psychology offers a possibility of understanding.

FUNDAMENTAL CONCEPTS
    1. *Tao*.
    2. Circular movement and the centre.

PHENOMENA OF THE WAY
    1. The disintegration of consciousness.
    2. *Animus* and *anima*.

THE DETACHMENT OF CONSCIOUSNESS FROM THE OBJECT.

THE FULFILMENT.

SUMMARY.

EXAMPLES OF EUROPEAN MAṆḌALAS.

INTRODUCTION

1. Difficulties encountered by a European in trying to understand the East

A thorough Westerner in feeling, I am necessarily deeply impressed by the strangeness of this Chinese text. It is true that a certain knowledge of Eastern religions and philosophies aids my intellect and intuition in understanding these ideas, partly at least, just as I can fathom the paradoxes of primitive religious ideas " ethnologically ", or as a matter of the " comparative history of religions ". This, in fact, is the Western way of hiding one's own heart under the cloak of so-called scientific understanding. We do it partly because of the *misérable vanité des savants* which fears and rejects with horror any sign of living sympathy, and partly because an understanding that reaches the feelings might allow contact with the foreign spirit to become a serious experience. So-called scientific objectivity would therefore have insisted on reserving this text for the philological acuity of sinologues, and would have guarded it jealously from any other interpretation. But Richard Wilhelm has penetrated too deeply into the secret and mysterious life of Chinese wisdom for him to have allowed such a pearl of great insight to be shelved by any one of the special sciences. It is an especial honour and pleasure that his choice of a psychological commentator has fallen upon me.

However, in this way, this rare piece of general knowledge runs the risk of being stowed away upon the shelf of yet another of the special sciences. Yet whoever seeks to minimize the merits of Western science is undermining the main support of the European mind. Science is not, indeed, a perfect instrument, but none the less it is an invaluable, superior one which only works harm when taken as an end in itself. Scientific method must serve; it errs when it usurps a throne. It must be ready to serve all branches of science, because each, by reason of its insufficiency, has need of support from the others. Science is the best tool of the Western mind and with it more doors can be opened than with bare hands. Thus it is part and parcel of our understanding and only clouds our insight when it lays claim to being the one and only way of comprehending. But it is the East that has taught us another, wider, more profound, and a higher understanding, that is, understanding through life. We know this way only vaguely, as a mere shadowy sentiment culled from religious terminology, and therefore we gladly dispose of Eastern " wisdom " in quotation marks, and push it away into the obscure territory of faith and superstition. But in this way Eastern " realism " is completely misunderstood. It does not consist of sentimental, exaggeratedly mystical, intuitions bordering on the pathological and emanating from ascetic recluses and cranks; the wisdom of the East is based on practical knowledge coming from the flower of Chinese intelligence, which we have not the slightest justification for undervaluing.

This assertion may, perhaps, seem extremely bold, and therefore will incite a certain amount of doubt, but, considering the extraordinary dearth of knowledge about the material, doubt is pardonable. Moreover, the strangeness of the material is so arresting that our embarrassment as to how and when the Chinese world of thought might be joined to ours, is quite understandable. When faced with this problem of grasping the ideas of the East, the usual mistake of the Western man is like that of the student in Faust. Ill-advised by the devil, he contemptuously turns his back on science, and, getting a whiff of eastern ecstatics, takes over their yoga practices quite literally, only to become a pitiable imitator. (Theosophy is our best example of this mistake.) And so he abandons the one safe foundation of the Western mind, and loses himself in a mist of words and ideas which never would have originated in European brains, and which can never be profitably grafted upon them.

An ancient adept has said: But if the wrong man uses the right means, the right means work in the wrong way. This Chinese saying, unfortunately all too true, stands in sharp contrast to our belief in the " right " method irrespective of the man who applies it. In reality, when it comes to things like these, everything depends on the man and little or nothing on the method. The latter is only the way and direction laid down by a man in order that his action may be the true expression of his nature. If it fails to be this, then the method is nothing more than an affectation, something artificially pieced on, rootless and sapless, serving only the illegitimate goal of self-deception. It becomes a means of fooling oneself and of evading what is perhaps the implacable law of one's being.

This has nothing whatever to do with the earth-born quality and sincerity of Chinese thought. On the contrary, it is the denial of one's own being, a self-betrayal to strange and unclean gods, a cowardly trick for the purpose of usurping psychic superiority, everything in fact, which is profoundly contrary to the meaning of Chinese " method ". Their views result from a way of life that is complete, genuine, and true in the fullest sense; they are views that come from that ancient, cultural life of China which has grown both logically and coherently from deep instincts, and which, for us, is forever remote and inimitable.

Western imitation of the East is doubly tragic in that it comes from a psychological misunderstanding as sterile as are the modern escapades in New Mexico, the blissful South Sea Islands, and Central Africa, where " primitivity" is being staged in all seriousness, in order that western civilized man may covertly slip out of his menacing duties, his *Hic Rhodus hic salta*. It is not for us to imitate what is organically foreign, or worse still, to send out missionaries to foreign peoples; it is our task to build up our own Western culture, which sickens with a thousand ills. This has to be done on the spot, and into the work must be drawn the real European as he is in his western commonplaceness, with his marriage problems, his neuroses, his social and political illusions, and his whole philosophical disorientation.

We should do well to confess at once, that, fundamentally speaking, we do not understand the utter unworldliness of a text like this, indeed, that we do not want to understand it. Have we, perhaps, an inkling that a mental attitude which can direct the glance inward to that extent owes its detachment from the world to the fact that those men have so completely fulfilled the instinctive demands of their natures that little or nothing prevents them from perceiving the invisible essence of the world ? Can it be, perhaps, that the condition of such knowledge is freedom from those desires, ambitions, and passions, which bind us to the visible world, and must not this freedom result from the intelligent fulfilment of instinctive demands, rather than from a premature repression, or one growing out of fear ? Do we only become free to know the world of the mind when the laws of earth have been obeyed? The man who knows the history of Chinese culture, and who besides has carefully studied the *I Ching*, that book of wisdom permeating all Chinese thought for thousands of years, will not lightly wave aside these doubts. He will know, moreover, that in the Chinese sense, the views set forth in our text are nothing extraordinary, but are quite unescapable, psychological conclusions.

For a long time, spirit, and the passion of the spirit, were the greatest values and the things most worth striving for in our peculiar Christian culture of the mind. Only after the decline of the Middle Ages, that is, in the course of the nineteenth century, when spirit began to degenerate into intellect, there set in a reaction against the unbearable domination of intellectualism which led to the pardonable mistake of confusing intellect with spirit, and blaming the latter for the misdeeds of the former. Intellect does, in fact, violate the soul when it tries to possess itself of the heritage of the spirit. It is in no way fitted to do this, because spirit is something higher than intellect in that it includes not only the latter, but the feelings as well. It is a line or principle of life that strives after superhuman, shining heights; but, in opposition to it, stands the dark, earth-born, feminine principle with its emotionality and instinctiveness reaching far back into the depths of time, and into the roots of physiological continuity. Without a doubt, these concepts are purely intuitive visions, but one cannot dispense with them if one tries to understand the nature of the human soul. China could not dispense with them because, as the history of Chinese philosophy shows, it has never gone so far from central psychic facts as to lose itself in a one-sided over-development and over-valuation of a single psychic function. Therefore, the Chinese have never failed to recognize the paradoxes and the polarity inherent in all life. The opposites always balance on the scales—a sign of high culture. Onesidedness, though it lends momentum, is a mark of barbarism. Therefore, I can only take the reaction which begins in the West against the intellect in favour of *eros*, and in favour of intuition, as a mark of cultural advance, a widening of consciousness beyond the too narrow limits set by a tyrannical intellect.

But it is far from my wish to undervalue the tremendous differentiation of western intellect, because, measured by it, eastern intellect can be described as childish. (Obviously this has nothing to do with intelligence.) If we should succeed in bringing another, or still a third function to the dignity accorded intellect, then the West could expect to surpass the East by a very great deal. It is therefore lamentable indeed when the European is false to himself and imitates the East or " affects " it in any way. He would have so much greater possibilities if he would remain true to himself and develop out of his own nature all that the East has brought forth from its inner being in the course of the centuries.

In general, and looked at from the incurably external point of view of the intellect, it will seem as if the things so highly valued by the East were not desirable for us. Above all, mere intellect cannot fathom the practical importance eastern ideas might have for us, and that is why it can classify these ideas as philosophical and ethnological curiosities and nothing more. The lack of comprehension goes so far, that even learned sinologues have not understood the practical application of the *I Ching*, and have therefore looked on the book as a collection of abstruse magic charms.

2. Modern Psychology offers a Possibility of Understanding

My experience in my practice has been such as to reveal to me a quite new and unexpected approach to eastern wisdom. But it must be well understood that I did not have as a starting point a more or less adequate knowledge of Chinese philosophy. On the contrary, when I began my life-work in the practice of psychiatry and psychotherapy, I was completely ignorant of Chinese philosophy, and it is only later that my professional experiences have shown me that in my technique I had been unconsciously led along that secret way which for centuries has been the preoccupation of the best minds of the East. This might have been taken for subjective imagination—one reason for my previous hesitancy in publishing anything on the subject—but Wilhelm, that expert authority on the soul of China, has openly confirmed the coincidence for me. In so doing, he has given me the courage to write about a Chinese text which, though belonging in essence to the mysterious shadows of the eastern mind, yet at the same time, and this is important, shows striking parallels to the course of psychic development in my patients, none of whom is Chinese.

In order to make this strange fact more intelligible to the reader, it must be mentioned that just as the human body shows a common anatomy over and above all racial differences, so too, does the psyche possess a common substratum. I have called the latter the collective unconscious. As a common human heritage it transcends all differences of culture and consciousness and does not consist merely of contents capable of becoming conscious, but of latent dispositions toward identical reactions. Thus the fact of the collective unconscious is simply the psychic expression of identity of brain-structure irrespective of all racial differences. By its means can be explained the analogy, going even as far as identity, between various myth-themes and symbols, and the possibility of human understanding in general. The various lines of psychic development start from one common stock whose roots reach back into the past. Here too lies the psychological parallelism with animals.

Taken purely psychologically, it means that we have common instincts of ideation (imagination), and of action. All conscious imagination and action have grown out of these unconscious prototypes, and remain bound up with them. Especially is this the case when consciousness has not attained any high degree of clarity, that is, when, in all its functions, it is more dependent on the instincts than on the conscious will, more governed by affect than by rational judgment. This condition ensures a primitive health of the psyche, which, however, immediately becomes lack of adaptiveness as soon as there arise circumstances that call for a higher moral effort. Instincts suffice only for a nature which, on the whole, remains on one level. An individual who is more guided by unconscious choice than by the conscious one, tends therefore toward outspoken psychic conservatism. This is the reason the primitive does not change in the course of thousands of years, and it is also the cause of his fearing everything strange and unusual. Were he less conservative, it might lead to maladaptation, and thus to the greatest of psychic dangers, namely a kind of neurosis. A higher and wider consciousness which only comes by means of assimilating the unfamiliar, tends toward autonomy, toward revolution against the old gods who are nothing other than those powerful, unconscious, primordial images which, up to this time, have held consciousness in thrall.

The more powerful and independent consciousness becomes, and with it the conscious will, the more is the unconscious forced into the background. When this happens, it becomes easily possible for the conscious structures to be detached from the unconscious images. Gaining thus in freedom, they break the chains of mere instinctiveness, and finally arrive at a state that is deprived of, or contrary to instinct. Consciousness thus torn from its roots and no longer able to appeal to the authority of the primordial images, possesses a Promethean freedom, it is true, but it also partakes of the nature of a godless *hybris*. It soars above the earth, even above mankind, but the danger of capsizing is there, not for every individual, to be sure, but collectively for the weak members of such a society, who again Promethean-like, are bound by the unconscious to the Caucasus. The wise Chinese would say in the words of the *I Ching* : When *yang* has reached its greatest strength, the dark power of *yin* is born within its depths ; night begins at midday when *yang* breaks up and begins to change into *yin*.

A physician is in a position to see this cycle of changes translated literally into life. He sees, for instance, a successful business man attaining all his desires regardless of death and the devil, and then withdrawing from activity at the crowning point of his success. In a short time the man falls into a neurosis, which changes him into a querulous old woman, fastens him to his bed, and thus finally destroys him. The picture is complete even to the change from the masculine to the feminine attitude. An exact parallel to this is the legend of Nebuchadnezzar in the book of Daniel, and the type of lunacy of Caesars in general. Similar cases of a one-sided exaggeration in the conscious standpoint, and of a corresponding *yin* reaction of the unconscious, form no small part of the practice of nerve specialists of our time, a time which so over-values the conscious will as to believe that " where there is a will there is a way ". Not that I wish to detract in the least from the high moral value of conscious willing ; consciousness and will should not be depreciated but should be considered as the greatest cultural achievements of humanity. But of what use is a morality that destroys humanity ? The bringing of will and capacity into harmony seems to me to be something more than morality. Morality *à tout prix*—a sign of barbarism— oftentimes wisdom is better ; but perhaps I look at this through the professional glasses of the physician who has to mend the ills following in the wake of an exaggerated cultural achievement.

Be that as it may. In any case, it is a fact that consciousness, increased by a necessary one-sidedness, gets so far out of touch with the primordial images as to make a collapse inevitable. Long before the actual catastrophe, the signs of the mistake announce themselves as absence of instinct, nervousness, disorientation, and entanglement in impossible situations and problems, etc. When the physician comes to investigate, he finds an unconscious which is in complete rebellion against the values of the conscious, and which, therefore, cannot possibly be assimilated to the conscious, while the reverse is altogether out of the question. One is then confronted with an apparently irreconcilable conflict with which human reason cannot deal except by sham solutions or dubious compromises. If both these evasions are rejected, one is faced with the question as to what has become of the much needed unity of personality, and with the necessity of seeking it. At this point begins the path travelled by the East since the beginning of things. Quite obviously, the Chinese owes the finding of this path, to the fact that he has never been led to force the pairs of opposites of human nature so far apart that all conscious connection between them was lost. The Chinese has this inclusive orientation because, as in the case of primitive mentality, the yea and the nay have remained in their original proximity. None the less, he could not escape feeling the collision of the opposites, and therefore he sought out the way of life in which he would be what the Hindu terms *nirdvandva*, free of the opposites.

Our text is concerned with this " Way ", and it is the question of this same " Way " that comes up with my patients also. There could be no greater mistake than for a Westerner to take up the direct practice of Chinese yoga, for then it would still be a matter of his will and consciousness, and would only strengthen the latter against the unconscious, bringing about the very effect which should have been avoided. The neurosis would then be increased. It cannot be sufficiently strongly emphasized that we are not orientals, and therefore have an entirely different point of departure in these things. It would also be a great mistake to assume that this is the path every neurotic must travel, or that it is the solution to be sought at every stage of the neurotic problem. It is appropriate only in those cases where the conscious has reached an abnormal degree of development, and has therefore diverged too far from the unconscious. This high degree of consciousness is the *conditio sine qua non*. Nothing would be more wrong than to wish to open this way to neurotics who are ill on account of the undue predominance of the unconscious. For the same reason, this way of development has scarcely any meaning before the middle of life (normally between the ages of thirty-five and forty), in fact, if entered upon too soon, it can be very injurious.

As has been indicated, the essential urge to find a

new way lay in the fact that the fundamental problem of the patient seemed insoluble to me unless violence was done to the one or the other side of his nature. I always worked with the temperamental conviction that in the last analysis there are no insoluble problems, and experience has so far justified me in that I have often seen individuals who simply outgrew a problem which had destroyed others. This " outgrowing ", as I called it previously, revealed itself on further experience to be the raising of the level of consciousness. Some higher or wider interest arose on the person's horizon, and through this widening of his view, the insoluble problem lost its urgency. It was not solved logically in its own terms, but faded out in contrast to a new and stronger life-tendency. It was not repressed and made unconscious, but merely appeared in a different light, and so became different itself. What, on a lower level, had led to the wildest conflicts and to emotions full of panic, viewed from the higher level of the personality, now seemed like a storm in the valley seen from a high mountain top. This does not mean that the thunderstorm is robbed of its reality; it means that, instead of being in it, one is now above it. But since, with respect to the psyche, we are both valley and mountain, it seems a vain illusion if one feels oneself to be above what is human. The individual certainly does feel the affect and is convulsed and tormented by it, yet at the same time he is aware of a higher consciousness which prevents him from being identical with the affect, a consciousness which takes the affect objectively, and can say, " I know that I suffer." Our text says of laziness : Laziness of which a man is conscious and laziness of which he is unconscious, are thousands of miles apart. In the highest degree this is true of affect also.

Here and there it happened in my practice that a patient grew beyond the dark possibilities within himself, and the observation of the fact was an experience of foremost importance to me. In the meantime, I had learned to see that the greatest and most important problems of life are all fundamentally insoluble. They must be so, because they express the necessary polarity inherent in every self-regulating system. They can never be solved, but only outgrown. I therefore asked myself whether this possibility of outgrowing, or further psychic development, was not normal, while to remain caught in a conflict was something pathological. Everyone must possess that higher level, at least in embryonic form, and in favourable circumstances, must be able to develop the possibility. When I examined the way of development of those persons who, quietly, and as if unconsciously, grew beyond themselves, I saw that their fates had something in common. Whether arising from without or within, the new thing came to all those persons from a dark field of possibilities; they accepted it and developed further by means of it. It seemed to me typical that, in some cases, the new thing was found outside themselves, and in others within; or rather, that it grew into some persons from without, and into others from within. But it was never something that came exclusively either from within or from without. If it came from outside the individual, it became an inner experience; if it came from within, it was changed into an outer event. But in no case was it conjured into existence through purpose and conscious willing, but rather seemed to flow out of the stream of time.

We are so greatly tempted to turn everything into purpose and method that I deliberately express myself in very abstract terms in order to avoid causing a prejudice in one direction or another. The new thing must not be pigeon-holed under any heading, for then it is applied in a way that permits mechanical duplication, and it would again be a case of the "right means" in the hands "of the wrong man". I have been deeply impressed with the fact that the new thing prepared by fate seldom or never corresponds to conscious expectation. It is a still more remarkable fact that, though the new thing contradicts deeply rooted instincts as we know them, yet it is a singularly appropriate expression of the total personality, an expression which one could not imagine in a more complete form.

What then did these people do in order to achieve the progress that freed them? As far as I could see they did nothing (*wu wei*),[1] but let things happen, for, as Master Lü Tzŭ teaches in our text, the Light circulates according to its own law, if one does not give up one's accustomed calling. The art of letting things happen, action in non-action, letting go of oneself, as taught by Master Eckehart, became a key to me with which I was able to open the door to the "Way". The key is this: we must be able to let things happen in the psyche. For us, this becomes a real art of which few people know anything. Consciousness is forever interfering, helping, correcting, and negating, and never leaving the simple growth of the psychic processes in peace. It would be a simple enough thing to do, if only simplicity were not the most difficult of all things. It consists solely in watching objectively the development of any fragment of fantasy. Nothing could be simpler than this, and yet right here the difficulties begin. Apparently no fantasy-fragment is at hand—yes there is one, but it is too stupid! Thousands of good excuses are brought against it: one cannot concentrate on it; it is too boring; what could come out of it? It is "nothing but, etc.". The conscious

[1] Inaction.

raises prolific objections, in fact, it often seems bent upon blotting out the spontaneous fantasy-activity despite the intention, nay, the firm determination of the individual, to allow the psychic processes to go forward without interference. In many cases there exists a veritable spasm of the conscious.

If one is successful in overcoming the initial difficulties, criticism is likely to start afterwards and attempt to interpret the fantasy, to classify, to æstheticize, or to depreciate it. The temptation to do this is almost irresistible. After a complete and faithful observation, free rein can be given to the impatience of the conscious; in fact it must be given, else obstructing resistances develop. But each time the fantasy-material is to be produced, the activity of the conscious must again be put aside.

In most cases the results of these efforts are not very encouraging at first. It is chiefly a matter of typical fantasy-material which admits of no clear statement as to whence it comes or whither it is going. Moreover, the way of getting at the fantasies is individually different. For many people, it is easiest to write them; others visualize them, and others again draw and paint them with or without visualization. In cases of a high degree of inflexibility in the conscious, oftentimes the hands alone can fantasy; they model or draw figures that are quite foreign to the conscious.

These exercises must be continued until the cramp in the conscious is released, or, in other words, until one can let things happen; which was the immediate goal of the exercise. In this way, a new attitude is created, an attitude which accepts the irrational and the unbelievable, simply because it is what is happening. This attitude would be poison for a person who has already been overwhelmed by things that just happen, but it is of the highest value for one who, with an exclusively conscious critique, chooses from the things that happen only those appropriate to his consciousness, and thus gets gradually drawn away from the stream of life into a stagnant backwater.

At this point, the way travelled by the two above-mentioned types seems to separate. Both have learned to accept what comes to them. (As Master Lü Tzü teaches: " When occupations come to us we must accept them; when things come to us we must understand them from the ground up.") One man will chiefly take what comes to him from without, and the other what comes from within, and, as determined by the law of life, the one will have to take from without something he never could accept from without, and the other will accept from within, things that always would have been excluded before.

This reversal of one's being means an enlargement, heightening, and enrichment of the personality when the previous values are adhered to along with the change, provided, of course, they are not mere illusions. If the values are not retained, the man goes over to the other side, and passes from fitness to unfitness, from adaptedness to the lack of it, from sense to nonsense, and from reason even to mental disease. The way is not without danger. Everything good is costly, and the development of the personality is one of the most costly of all things. It is a question of yea-saying to oneself, of taking the self as the most serious of tasks, keeping conscious of everything done, and keeping it constantly before one's eyes in all its dubious aspects—truly a task that touches us to the core.

The Chinese can fall back upon the authority of his

entire culture. If he starts on the long way, he does what is recognized as being the best of all the things he could do. But the Westerner who seriously wishes to start upon this way has all authority against him in intellectual, moral, and religious fields. Therefore it is infinitely easier for a man to imitate the Chinese method, and leave behind him the dubious European in himself. Or, choosing something less easy, he can seek again the way back to the mediævalism of the Christian Church, and build once more the European wall which is intended to shield true Christian men from the poor heathen and the ethnographic curiosities of the world. The æsthetic, or intellectual flirtation with life and fate comes to an abrupt end here. The step to higher consciousness leads away from all shelter and safety. The person must give himself to the new way completely, for it is only by means of his integrity that he can go farther, and only his integrity can guarantee that his way does not turn out to be an absurd adventure.

Whether a person receives his fate from without or from within, the experiences and events of the way remain the same. Therefore I need say nothing about the manifold outer and inner events, the endless variety of which I could never exhaust. Moreover, to do so would be meaningless in relation to the text under discussion. On the other hand, there is much to be said of the psychic conditions that accompany the further development. These psychic conditions are expressed symbolically in our text, and in the very symbols which, for many years, have been well-known to me in my practice.

THE FUNDAMENTAL CONCEPTS
1. TAO

The great difficulty in interpreting this and similar texts [1] for the European mind is due to the fact that the Chinese author always starts from the centre of things, from the point we would call his objective or goal; in a word, he begins with the ultimate insight he has set out to attain. Thus the Chinese author begins his work with ideas that demand a most comprehensive understanding on our part. So much so, that a man with a critical intellect feels he speaks with laughable pretension, or even that he is guilty of utter nonsense, if he dares launch a purely intellectual discourse on the subtle psychic experiences of the great minds of the East. For example, our text begins: "That which exists through itself, is called *Tao*." The *Hui Ming Ching* begins with the words: "The most subtle secret of *Tao* is essence and life."

It is characteristic of the Western mind that it has no concept for *Tao*. The Chinese sign is made up of the sign for "head", and that for "going". Wilhelm translates *Tao* by *Sinn* (Meaning). Others translate it as "Way", "Providence", or even as "God", as the Jesuits do. This shows the difficulty. "Head" could be taken as consciousness,[2] and "to go", as travelling a way, and then the idea would be: to go consciously, or the conscious way. This agrees with the fact that "the Light of Heaven" which "dwells between

---

[1] Compare Liu Hua-yang: *Hui Ming Ching, Das Buch von Bewusstsein und Leben*, (*The Book of Consciousness and Life*), translated into German by L. C. Lo, *Chinesische Blätter*, No. 1, vol. 3, published by Richard Wilhelm.

[2] The head is also the "seat of Heavenly Light".

the eyes" as the "Heart of Heaven", is used synonymously with *Tao*. "Essence and life" are contained in the "Light of Heaven", and according to Liu Hua-yang, are the most important secrets of *Tao*. "Light" is the symbolical equivalent of consciousness, and the nature of consciousness is expressed by analogies with light. The *Hui Ming Ching* is introduced with the verse:—

> "If thou wouldst complete the diamond body without emanations,
> Diligently heat the roots of consciousness[1] and life.
> Kindle Light in the blessed country ever close at hand,
> And, there hidden, let thy true self eternally dwell."

These verses contain a sort of alchemistic instruction as to a method or way of creating the "diamond body" which also appears in our text. "Heating" is necessary; that is, there must be a heightening of consciousness in order that the dwelling place of the spirit can be "illumined". But not only consciousness, life itself must be heightened. The union of these two produces "conscious life". According to the *Hui Ming Ching*, the ancient sages knew how to bridge the gap between consciousness and life because they cultivated both. In this way the immortal body is "melted out", and in this way "the great *Tao* is completed".[2]

If we take *Tao* as the method or conscious way by which to unite what is separated, we have probably come quite close to the psychological content of the concept. In any case, the separation of consciousness from life could not very well be understood as anything other than what I have described above as the deflection, or deracination of consciousness. Without doubt also, the question of

[1] In the *Hui Ming Ching*, "essence" and "consciousness" are used interchangeably.
[2] l.c., p. 104.

making the opposites conscious ("conversion"), means reunion with the laws of life represented in the unconscious, and the purpose of this reunion is the attainment of conscious life, or, expressed in Chinese terms, the bringing about of *Tao*.

2. THE CIRCULAR MOVEMENT AND THE CENTRE

As has already been pointed out, the union of the opposites [1] on a higher level of consciousness, is not a rational affair, nor is it a matter of will, but a psychic process of development which expresses itself in symbols. Historically, this process has always been represented in symbols, and to-day the development of individual personality is still rendered visible by symbolical figures. This fact was revealed to me through the following observations. The spontaneous fantasies of which we treated above, become more profound and concentrate themselves gradually around abstract structures which apparently represent "principles", true gnostic *archai*. When the fantasies are chiefly expressed in thoughts, the results are intuitive formulations of the dimly felt laws or principles, and these tend to be dramatized or personified. (We shall have to deal with these again later.) If the fantasies are drawn, there appear symbols that are chiefly of the so-called *mandala* [2] type. *Mandala* means a circle, more especially a magic circle, and this form of symbol is not only to be found all through the East, but also among us ; *mandalas* are amply represented in the Middle Ages. The specifically Christian ones come from the earlier Middle Ages. Most

---

[1] Compare my discussion in *Psychological Types*, chap. v.
[2] For a discussion of the *mandala*, see *Kunstform und Yoga im Indischen Kultbild*, Heinrich Zimmer, Frankfurter-Verlagsanstalt, Berlin, 1926.

of them show Christ in the centre, with the four evangelists, or their symbols, at the cardinal points. This conception must be a very ancient one because Horus was represented with his four sons in the same way by the Egyptians.[1] (It is known that Horus with his four sons was closely connected with Christ and the four evangelists.) Later there is to be found a clear and very interesting *mandala* in Jacob Boehme's book on the soul.[2] This latter *mandala*, it is easy to see, deals with a psycho-cosmic system having a strong Christian colour. Boehme calls it the " philosophical eye ",[3] or the " mirror of wisdom ", which obviously means a body of secret knowledge. For the most part, the *mandala* form is that of a flower, cross, or wheel, with a distinct tendency toward four as the basis of structure. (One is reminded of the *tetraktys*, the fundamental number in the Pythagorean system.) *Mandālas* of this sort are also to be found in the sand drawings used in the ceremonies of the Pueblo Indians.[4] But the most beautiful *mandalas* are, of course, those of the East, especially those belonging to Tibetan Buddhism. The symbols of our text are represented in these *mandalas*. I have also found *mandala* drawings among the mentally diseased, and they were patients who certainly did not have the least idea of any of the connections we have discussed.[5]

Among my patients I have come across cases of women who did not draw *mandala* symbols but who danced them instead. In India this type is called *mandala*

---

[1] Compare Wallis Budge, *The Gods of the Egyptians*.
[2] *For Forty Questions of the Soule.* 1602, first English translation.
[3] Compare the Chinese concept of the Heavenly Light between the eyes.
[4] Matthews, *The Mountain Chant*. Fifth Annual Report of the Bureau of Ethnology, 1883–4, and Stevenson, *Ceremonial of Hasjelti Dailjiis*, Eighth Annual Report of the Bureau of Ethnology, 1886–7.
[5] I have published the *mandala* of a somnambulist in *Collected Papers on Analytical Psychology*.

nrithya or *maṇḍala* dance, and the dance figures express the same meanings as the drawings. My patients can say very little about the meaning of the symbols but are fascinated by them and find them in some way or other expressive and effective with respect to the subjective psychic condition represented.

Our text promises to " reveal the secret of the Golden Flower of the Great *One* ". The Golden Flower is the Light, and the Light of Heaven is *Tao*. The Golden Flower is a *maṇḍala* symbol which I have often met with in the material brought me by my patients. It is drawn either (seen from above) as a regular geometric ornament, or as a flower growing from a plant. The plant is frequently a structure in brilliant fiery colours and is shown growing out of a bed of darkness, and carrying the blossom of light at the top, a symbol similar to that of the Christmas tree. But a drawing of this kind expresses more than the form of the Golden Flower; it suggests its origin as well, since according to the *Hui Ming Ching*, the " germinal vesicle " is the " dragon castle on the floor of the sea ". This vesicle is nothing other than the " golden castle ", the " Heavenly Heart ", the " terrace of life ", the " field of the square-inch ", the " house of the square-foot ", the " purple hall of the city of jade ", the " dark pass ", in the " space of former Heaven ". The list of richly significant names is not yet exhausted, for the " germinal vesicle " is also known as the " borderline of the snow mountains ", the " primordial pass ", the " empire of the greatest joy ", the " land without boundaries ", and " the altar upon which consciousness and life are made ". " If a dying man does not know this seed place," says the *Hui Ming Ching*, " he will not find the unity of consciousness and life in a thousand births and ten thousand æons."

The beginning, in which everything is still unity, and which therefore appears as the highest goal, lies on the floor of the sea in the darkness of the unconscious. In the germinal vesicle, life and consciousness (or " essence " and " life ", *hsing-ming*), are still a " unity ",[1] " inseparably mixed like the seeds of fire in the refining furnace." " Inside the germinal vesicle is the fire of the ruler." " In the germinal vesicle all wise men have begun their work." Note the fire analogies. I know a series of European *maṇḍala* drawings in which something like a plant seed surrounded with membranes is shown floating in water, and, from the depths below, fire penetrating the seed, makes it grow, and causes the formation of a large golden flower from within the germinal vesicle.

This symbolism refers to a sort of alchemic process of refining and " ennobling " ; darkness gives birth to light ; out of the " lead of the water-region ", grows the " noble " gold ; the unconscious becomes conscious in the form of a process of life and growth. (Hindu *Kundalini* yoga [2] affords a complete analogy.) In this way the union of consciousness and life takes place.

When my patients produce these *maṇḍala* pictures it is, of course, not through suggestion ; similar pictures were being made long before I knew their meaning or their connection with the strange practices of the East, which, at that time, were wholly unfamiliar to me. The pictures came quite spontaneously and from two sources. One source is the unconscious, which spontaneously produces such fantasies ; the other source is life, which, if lived with complete devotion, brings an intuition of the self, the individual being. When one becomes aware

[1] *Hui Ming Ching*, p. 105.
[2] Avalon, *The Serpent Power*. Luzac and Co., London, 1919.

of the latter, it is expressed in drawings, while the unconscious enforces an acceptance of life. Moreover, quite in accord with the Eastern conception, the *mandala* symbol is not only a means of expression, but works an effect. It reacts upon its maker. Very ancient magical effects are associated with this symbol because it comes originally from the " enclosing circle ", the " charmed circle ", the magic of which has been preserved in countless folk-customs.[1] The picture has the obvious purpose of drawing a *sulcus primigenius*, a magical furrow around the centre, the *templum*, or *temenos* (sacred precincts), of the innermost personality, in order to prevent " emanation ", or to guard by apotropæic means, deflections through external influences. Magical practices are nothing but the projections of psychic events, which, in cases like these, exert a counter influence on the soul, and act like a kind of enchantment of one's own personality. That is to say, by means of these concrete performances, the attention, or better said, the interest, is brought back to an inner, sacred domain, which is the source and goal of the soul. This inner domain contains the unity of life and consciousness, which, though once possessed, has been lost, and must now be found again.

The union of these two, life and consciousness, is *Tao*, whose symbol would be the central white light (compare the *Bardo Tödol*),[2] and the dwelling place of the light is the " quadrant ", or the " face ", that is, the space between the eyes. By means of these symbols it is intended to make visible the " creative point ", or that which has intensity without extension. It is a point conceived to be connected with the space of the " square-inch ", which is the symbol for that which has extension.

[1] I refer to the excellent collection of Knuchel, *Die Umwandlung in Kult, Magie und Rechtsgebrauch.*
[2] Evans-Wentz, *The Tibetan Book of the Dead*, 1927.

The two together make *Tao*. Essence, or consciousness (*hsing*), is expressed in light symbolism, and is therefore intensity, while life (*ming*), would coincide with extensity. The first has the character of the *yang* principle, the latter of the *yin*. The above-mentioned *maṇḍala* of a somnambulist girl, $15\frac{1}{2}$ years old, whom I had under observation thirty years ago, shows in its centre, a "spring of life-force" without extension, which in its emanations collides directly with its contradictory space-principle, thus bringing the symbolism into complete analogy with the fundamental idea of the Chinese.

The "enclosure", or *circumambulatio* is expressed in our text by the idea of a "circular course". The "circular course" is not merely motion in a circle, but means, on the one side, the marking off of the sacred precinct, and, on the other, fixation and concentration. The sunwheel begins to run; that is to say, the sun is activated, and begins to take its course, or, in other words, *Tao* begins to be effective and to take the leadership. Action is reversed into non-action; all that is peripheral is subjected to the command of the centre. Therefore it is said: Movement is only another name for mastery. Psychologically, this circular course would be the "turning in a circle about oneself", by means of which, apparently, all sides of the personality become implicated. "The poles of Light and Darkness are made to rotate; there comes a change from day to night."

"*Es wechselt Paradiesehelle*[1]
Mit tiefer, schauervoller Nacht."

Thus the circular movement has also the moral significance of activating all the light and dark forces of human nature, and with them, all the psychological opposites of whatever kind they may be. That means

[1] "The radiance of Paradise alternates with deep, dreadful night." (*Faust.*)

nothing else than self-knowledge by means of self-incubation (Hindu *tapas*). A similar primordial concept of an absolutely complete creature is that of the Platonic man, round on all sides and uniting within himself the two sexes.

One of the finest parallels to what has been said here, is the description of his central experience given by Edward Maitland, the co-worker of Anna Kingsford.[1] As far as possible I have followed his own words. He had discovered that during reflection on an idea, related ideas became visible, so to speak, in a long series, apparently back to their source, which to him was the divine spirit. By means of concentration on the series, he made the effort to press on to their origin. He says : " I was absolutely without knowledge or expectation when I yielded to the impulse to make the attempt. I simply experimented on a faculty . . . being seated at my writing-table the while in order to record the results as they came, and resolved to retain my hold on my outer and circumferential consciousness, no matter how far towards my inner and central consciousness I might go. For I knew not whether I should be able to regain the former if I once quitted my hold of it, or to recollect the facts of the experience. At length I achieved my object, though only by a strong effort, the tension occasioned by the endeavour to keep both extremes of the consciousness in view at once being very great."

" Once well started on my quest, I found myself traversing a succession of spheres or belts . . . the impression produced being that of mounting a vast ladder stretching from the circumference towards the centre of a system, which was at once my own system, the solar system, and the universal system, the three systems being

[1] I am indebted for this reference to my esteemed colleague, Dr. Beatrice Hinkle, of New York. The title reads : *Anna Kingsford, Her Life, Letters, Diary, and Work*, by Edward Maitland, Redway, London, 1896. Note especially page 129 f.

at once diverse and identical. . . . Presently, by a supreme, and what I felt must be a final, effort . . . I succeeded in polarizing the whole of the convergent rays of my consciousness into the desired focus. And at the same instant, as if through the sudden ignition of the rays thus fused into a unity, I found myself confronted with a glory of unspeakable whiteness and brightness, and of a lustre so intense as well-nigh to beat me back. . . . But though feeling that I had no need to explore further, I resolved to make assurance doubly sure by piercing if I could the almost blinding lustre, and seeing what it enshrined. With a great effort I succeeded, and the glance revealed to me that which I had felt must be there. . . . It was the dual form of the Son . . . the unmanifest made manifest, the unformulate formulate, the unindividuate individuate, God as the Lord, proving through His duality that God is Substance as well as Force, Love as well as Will, Feminine as well as Masculine, Mother as well as Father." He found that God is two in one like man. Beside this he noticed something that our text also emphasizes, namely, " suspension of breathing." He says ordinary breathing stopped and was replaced by an internal respiration, " as if by the breathing of a distinct personality within and other than the physical organism." He took this being to be the entelechy of Aristotle, and the inner Christ of the Apostle Paul, the " spiritual and substantial individuality engendered within the physical and phenomenal personality, and representing, therefore, the rebirth of the man on a plane transcending the material ".

This genuine [1] experience contains all the essential

---

[1] Such experiences are genuine, but their genuineness does not prove that all the conclusions or convictions forming their context are necessarily sound. Even in cases of lunacy one comes across perfectly valid psychic experiences. (C. G. J.)

symbols of our text. The phenomenon itself, that is the light-vision, is an experience common to many mystics, and one that is undoubtedly of the greatest significance, because in all times and places it appears as the unconditional thing, which unites in itself the greatest power and the profoundest meaning. Hildegarde von Bingen, a significant personality quite apart from her mysticism, expresses herself about her central vision in a quite similar way. " Since my childhood," she says, " I always see a light in my soul, but not with the outer eyes, nor through the thoughts of my heart; neither do the five outer senses take part in this vision. . . . The light I perceive is not of a local kind, but is much brighter than the cloud which bears the sun. I cannot distinguish in it height, breadth, or length. . . . What I see or learn in such a vision stays long in my memory. I see, hear, and know at the same time, and learn what I know in the same moment. . . . I cannot recognize any sort of form in this light, although I sometimes see in it another light that is known to me as the living light. . . . While I am enjoying the spectacle of this light, all sadness and sorrow disappear from my memory . . ."

I know a few individuals who are familiar with this phenomenon from personal experience. As far as I have ever been able to understand it, the phenomenon seems to have to do with an acute condition of consciousness as intensive as it is abstract, a " detached " consciousness (see below), which, as Hildegarde pertinently remarks, brings up to consciousness regions of psychic events ordinarily covered with darkness. The fact that, in connection with this, the general bodily sensations disappear, shows that their specific energy has been withdrawn from them, and has apparently gone toward heightening the clearness of consciousness. As a rule, the phenomenon is spontaneous, coming and going on its own initiative. Its effect is astonishing in that it almost always brings about a solution of psychic complications, and thereby frees the inner personality from emotional and imaginary entanglements, creating thus a unity of being, which is universally felt as a " release ".

The achievement of such a symbolic unity is beyond the power of the conscious will because, in this case, the conscious is partisan. Its opponent is the collective unconscious which does not understand the language of the conscious. Therefore it is necessary to have the " magically " effective symbol which contains those primitive analogies that speak to the unconscious. The unconscious can only be reached and expressed by the symbol, which is the reason why the process of individuation can never do without the symbol. The symbol is, on the one hand, the primitive expression of the unconscious, while, on the other hand, it is an idea corresponding to the highest intuition produced by consciousness.

The oldest *maṇḍala* known to me, is a palæolithic so-called " sunwheel ", recently discovered in Rhodesia. It is likewise founded on the principle of four. Things reaching so far back in human history naturally touch upon the deepest layers of the unconscious and make it possible to grasp the latter where conscious speech shows itself to be quite impotent. Such things cannot be thought out but must grow again from the forgotten depths, if they are to express the supreme presentiments of consciousness and the loftiest intuitions of the spirit. Coming from these depths they can unite the uniqueness of present-day consciousness with the age-old past of life.

PHENOMENA OF THE WAY

1. The Disintegration of Consciousness

Danger arises whenever the narrowly delimited, but intensely clear, individual consciousness meets the immense expansion of the collective unconscious, because the latter has a definitely disintegrating effect on consciousness. According to the exposition of the *Hui Ming Ching*, this effect belongs to the peculiar phenomena of Chinese yoga practice. It is said there [1]: Every thought-fragment takes shape and becomes visible in colour and form. All the powers of the soul reveal their traces.[2] One of the illustrations [3] accompanying the book shows a sage sunk in contemplation, his head circled with fire, out of which five human figures emerge: these five split up again into twenty-five smaller figures. That would represent a schizophrenic process if it remained a permanent condition. Therefore the instructions, as though warning the adept, say: Figures formed out of the fire of the spirit, are only empty colours and forms. The Light of the essence streams back to the primordial truth.

It is understandable then why the protecting figure of the " enclosing circle " was seized upon. It is intended to prevent " emanations ", and to protect the unity of consciousness from being split apart by the unconscious. Moreover, the Chinese concept points a way toward lessening

---

[1] *L.c.*, p. 112.

[2] Here belong also the recurrent memories of earlier incarnations that arise during contemplation.

[3] This picture and the others of the series in the *Hui Ming Ching* have been reproduced by Wilhelm and appear in this book. (C. F. B.)

the disintegrating effect of the unconscious; it describes the "thought-figures" or "thought-fragments" as "empty colours and shapes", and thus depotentializes them as far as that is possible. This idea goes through the whole of Buddhism (especially the *Mahāyāna* form), and, in the instructions to the dead of the *Bardo Tödol*, it is even pushed to the point of explaining both favourable and unfavourable gods as illusions still to be overcome.

It certainly is not within the competence of the psychologist to establish the metaphysical truth or falsity of this idea; he must be content to determine wherever possible what is psychically effective. In doing this, he need not bother himself as to whether the shape in question is a transcendental illusion or not, since faith, not science, has to decide this point. We are working here in a field which for a long time has seemed to be outside the domain of science, and which has therefore been looked upon as altogether illusory. But there is no scientific justification for such an assumption, because the substantiality of these things is not a scientific problem since, in any case, it lies beyond the power of human perception and criticism, and therefore beyond any possibility of proof. The psychologist is not concerned with the substance of these complexes, but with the psychic experiences. Without a doubt they are psychic contents which can be experienced, and which have an indisputable autonomy. They are psychic partial-systems which either appear spontaneously in ecstatic condition and cause powerful impressions and effects, or else become fixed as mental disturbances in the form of lunacies and hallucinations, thus destroying the unity of the personality.

The psychiatrist is always prone to believe in toxins and the like, and to explain schizophrenia (splitting of the mind in a psychosis) in these terms, leaving the psychic contents out of account. On the other hand, in psychogenetic disturbances (hysteria, compulsion neurosis, etc.), where the question of toxic effects and cell degeneration cannot possibly arise, there are to be found, in somnambulistic conditions for example, independent, split-off complexes. Freud would explain these as due to unconscious repression of sexuality, but this explanation is by no means valid for all cases, because there can evolve spontaneously out of the unconscious, contents which the conscious cannot assimilate, and, in such cases, the repression hypothesis is inadequate. Moreover, the essential autonomy of these elements can be observed in the effects of daily life which obstinately obtrude themselves against our wills, and then, despite our most desperate efforts toward repression, overwhelm the ego and force it under their control. No wonder that the primitive sees in these moods either a state of possession, or sets them down to the loss of a soul. Our colloquial speech reflects the same thing when we say : " I don't know what has got into him to-day "; "He is ridden by the devil"; "It has him again"; "He was beside himself"; "He behaves as if possessed." Even legal practice recognizes a partial lessening of responsibility in a state of affect. Autonomic psychic contents are therefore quite common experiences for us, and such contents have a disintegrating effect on the conscious.

But besides the ordinary, widely recognized affects, there are subtler, more complex emotional states which cannot be described as pure and simple affects but are complicated partial-systems which have more of the character of personalities the more complicated they are. Being also constituents of the psychic personality, they necessarily have the character of persons. Such partial-systems appear in mental diseases where there is no psychogenetic splitting of the personality (double personality), and also, quite commonly, in mediumistic phenomena. They are also encountered in the religious phenomena, and therefore many of the earlier gods have developed from persons to personified ideas, and finally into abstract ideas. As we know, activated unconscious contents always appear first as projections upon the outside world. In the course of mental development, consciousness gradually assimilates them and reshapes them into conscious ideas which then forfeit their originally autonomous and personal character. Some of the old gods, after serving as carriers of astrological projections, became mere descriptive attributes (martial, jovial, saturnine, erotic, logical, lunatic, etc.).

The instructions of the *Bardo Tödol*, especially, enable us to see how greatly the conscious is threatened with disintegration through these figures. Again and again, the dead are instructed not to take these shapes as real, and not to confuse their gloomy appearance with the pure white light of *Dharmakāya* ("the divine body of truth"). The meaning is that they are not to project the one light of highest consciousness into concretized figures, and in such a way dissolve into a plurality of autonomous partial-systems. If there were no danger in this, and if the partial-systems were not menacingly autonomous and divergent tendencies, such urgent instructions would not be necessary. If we consider the simpler, polytheistically orientated attitude of the Eastern man, these instructions are almost as significant as would be warnings to a Christian not to let himself be blinded by the illusion of a personal God, not to mention a Trinity and innumerable angels and saints.

If tendencies toward splitting were not inherent characteristics of the human psyche, partial-systems would never have been separated off. In other words, there would never have been either spirits or gods. That is the reason, too, that our time is so utterly godless and profane, lacking as we do knowledge of the unconscious psyche, and pursuing an exclusive cult of consciousness. Our true religion is a monotheism of consciousness, a possession by it, with a fanatical denial of the existence of autonomous partial-systems. In this we differ from the Buddhist yoga doctrine, because we even deny that partial-systems can be experienced. Since the repressed material appears again in consciousness in unsuitable form, a great psychic danger arises here, because the partial-systems then behave like any other repressed contents, and induce compulsive, wrong attitudes. This fact, which is so striking in every case of neurosis, holds true also for the collective psychic phenomena. In this respect, our time is caught in a fatal error; we believe we can criticize religious facts intellectually; we think, for instance, like Laplace, that God is a hypothesis which can be subjected to intellectual treatment, affirmation, or denial. It is completely forgotten that the reason humanity believed in " dæmons " has nothing whatever to do with anything external, but depends entirely on naïve awareness of the powerful inner effect of autonomous partial-systems. This effect is not stopped by criticizing its name intellectually, nor by describing it as false. The effect is collectively always present; the autonomous systems are always at work, because the fundamental structure of the unconscious is not disturbed by the fluctuations of a transitory consciousness.

If one denies the existence of the partial-systems, hoping to be rid of them by a criticism of the name, then their effect, which nevertheless continues, cannot be understood, and therefore they cannot be assimilated to consciousness. They then become an inexplicable factor of disturbance which one assumes to exist somewhere or other outside. In this way, there results a projection of the partial-system, and, at the same time, a dangerous situation is created, because the disturbing effects are now attributed to a bad will outside ourselves which is perforce located at our neighbour's " *de l'autre côté de la rivière* ". This leads to collective delusions, instigations to war and revolution, in a word, to destructive mass psychoses.

Insanity is possession by an unconscious content which, as such, is not assimilated to consciousness, nor can it be assimilated, since consciousness has denied the existence of such contents. Religiously expressed, the attitude is equivalent to saying : " We no longer have any fear of God and believe that everything is to be measured in terms of human standards." This *hybris*, that is, this narrowness of consciousness, is always the shortest way to the insane asylum. I recommend the excellent presentation of this problem in H. G. Wells' novel, *Christina Alberta's Father*, and Schreber's *Denkwürdigkeiten eines Nervenkranken*.[1]

It must stir a sympathetic chord in an enlightened European when it is said in the *Hui Ming Ching* that the " shapes formed from the fire of the spirit are only empty colours and forms ". That sounds quite European and seems to suit our reason excellently. We, indeed, think we can flatter ourselves at having already reached such heights of clarity because such phantoms of gods seem to have been left far behind. But the things we have outgrown are only the word-ghosts, not the psychic facts which were responsible for the birth of the gods. We are just as much possessed by our autonomous psychic

[1] Mutze, Leipzig.

contents as if they were gods. To-day they are called phobias, compulsions, etc., or briefly, neurotic symptoms. The gods have become diseases; not Zeus, but the solar plexus, now rules Olympus and causes the oddities of the professional office hour, or disturbs the brains of the politician and journalist who then unwittingly release mental epidemics.

Therefore it is better for the Western man not to know too much about the secret insight of Eastern wise men, because it would then be a case of the " right means in the hands of the wrong men ". Instead of again convincing himself that the dæmon is an illusion, the Westerner ought to experience the reality of this illusion again. He ought to learn to recognize these psychic powers again, and not wait until his moods, nervous states, and insane ideas, make clear to him in the most painful possible way that he is not the only master in his house. The splitting tendencies are effective psychic personalities of a relative reality. They are real when they are not recognized as real and are therefore projected; relatively real when they are related to the conscious (in religions this stage leads to the forming of a cult); but they are unreal in so far as consciousness has begun to detach itself from its contents.

However, the latter is only the case when life has been lived so exhaustively, and with such devotion, that no more unfulfilled life-duties exist, and when, therefore, there are no more desires which cannot be sacrificed without hesitation. In a word, this detachment of consciousness can only begin when nothing remains to prevent an inner superiority to the world. It is futile to lie to oneself about this. Wherever one is caught, one is still possessed; and, when one is possessed, it means the presence of something stronger than oneself. (" Truly from thence will't thou ne'er come forth until thou hast paid the last farthing.") It is not a matter of unconcern whether one calls something a "mania" or a "god". To serve a mania is detestable and undignified, but to serve a god is full of meaning, and rich in possibilities because it means yielding to a higher, invisible, and spiritual being. The personification enables one to see the relative reality of the autonomous partial-system, which, in turn, makes its assimilation possible and depotentializes the forces of external life. When God is not recognized, selfish desires develop, and out of this selfishness comes illness.

Yoga teaching assumes the recognition of gods to be something granted. Its secret instruction is therefore only intended for him whose light of consciousness is capable of freeing him from the powers of life, in order to enter into the ultimate undivided unity, into the "centre of emptiness", where "dwells the god of utmost emptiness and life", as our text says. "To hear such a teaching is difficult to attain in thousands of æons." Obviously, the veil of *Maya* cannot be lifted by a mere decision of reason, but demands the most thoroughgoing and wearisome preparation consisting in the right payment of all debts to life. For, as long as one is in any way held by the domination of *cupiditas*, the veil is not lifted, and the heights of a consciousness, empty of content and free of illusion, are not reached, nor can any trick nor any deceit bring it about. It is an ideal that can only be completely realized in death. Till then, there are real, and relatively real, figures of the unconscious.

2. ANIMUS AND ANIMA

According to our text there belong to the figures of the unconscious, not only gods, but also the *animus* and *anima*. The word *hun* is translated by Wilhelm as *animus*. As a matter of fact, the concept *animus* seems very appropriate for *hun*, the character for which is made up of the character for " clouds " and that for " dæmon ". *Hun* means, then, " cloud-dæmon," a higher, spirit-soul belonging to the *yang* principle and therefore masculine. After death, *hun* rises above and becomes *shên*, the " expanding and revealing " spirit or god. The *anima*, called *p'o*, and written with the character for " white ", and that for " dæmon", that is, " white ghost ", belongs to the lower, earth-bound, bodily soul, partakes of the *yin* principle, and is therefore feminine. After death, it sinks and becomes *kuei* (dæmon), often explained as the " one who returns " (i.e. to earth), a *revenant*, a ghost. The fact that the *animus* as well as the *anima* part after death and go their ways independently, shows that, for the Chinese consciousness, they are separable psychic factors which have markedly different effects, and, despite the fact that originally they are united in " one effective, true essence ", in the " house of the creative ", they are two. " The *animus* is in the Heavenly Heart; by day it lives in the eyes (that is in consciousness); at night it dreams away in the liver." It is that " which we have received from the great emptiness, that which has form from the very beginning ". The *anima*, on the other hand, is the " force of heaviness and sadness " ; it clings to the bodily, fleshly heart. " Moods and impulses to anger " are its effects. " Whoever is dull and moody on waking, is fettered by the *anima*."

Many years ago, before Wilhelm made me acquainted

with this text, I used the concept *anima* [1] in a way quite analogous to the Chinese definition of *p'o*, and of course entirely apart from any metaphysical premise. To the psychologist, the *anima* is not a transcendental being but something quite within the range of experience. As the Chinese definition also makes clear, affective conditions are immediate experiences. But why does one speak of *anima* and not simply of moods? The reason for this is that affects have an autonomous character, and therefore most people are under their power. But, as we have seen, affects are delimitable contents of consciousness, parts of the personality, in other words. As parts of the personality, they partake of its character, and can therefore be easily personified, a process which is still going on to-day, as the examples cited above have shown. The personification is not an idle invention, inasmuch as the individual stirred by affect does not show a vague, but a quite definite, character, different from his ordinary one. Careful investigation has shown that the affective character in a man has feminine traits. From this psychological fact comes the Chinese teaching of the *p'o*-soul, as well as my concept of the *anima*. Deeper introspection, or ecstatic experience, reveals the existence of a feminine figure in the unconscious, therefore the feminine name, *anima*, *psyche*, *âme*, *Seele*. The *anima* can also be defined as an image, or archetype, or as the resultant of all the experiences of man with woman. This is the reason the *anima* image is projected on the woman. Poetry, as is well known, has often described and celebrated the *anima*.[2] The relation of the *anima* to the spook in the Chinese concept is interesting to

[1] I refer the reader to the comprehensive presentation in my book, *Two Essays on Analytical Psychology*. Baillère, Tyndall, and Cox, London.
[2] *Psychological Types*, chap. v.

parapsychologists in that the "controls" are very often of the opposite sex.

Although I cannot but approve Wilhelm's translation of *hun* by *animus*, as being a perfectly good philological equivalent, none the less I had very important reasons for choosing the expression *logos* for a man's mental essence, his clarity of consciousness and reason. Chinese philosophers are spared certain difficulties which burden the task of Western psychologists, because Chinese philosophy, like all mental and spiritual activity of ancient times, is the exclusive constituent of the man's world. Its concepts are never taken psychologically, and have therefore never been examined as to how far they also apply to the feminine psyche. But the psychologist cannot possibly ignore the existence of woman and her peculiar psychology. This is the reason I prefer to translate *hun* as it appears in a man, by *logos*. Wilhelm in his translation uses *logos* for the Chinese concept *hsing*, which could also be translated as *essence*, or *creative consciousness*. After death, *hun* becomes *shên*, spirit, which is very close, in the philosophical sense, to *hsing*. Since the Chinese concepts are not logical in our sense, but are intuitive perceptions, their meaning can only be fathomed through the ways in which they are used, and by noting the constitution of the written signs, or further, by such relationships as that of *hun* to *shên*. *Hun*, then, would be the discriminating light of consciousness and of reason in man, originally coming from the *logos spermatikos* of *hsing*, and returning after death through *shên* to *Tao*. Used this way the expression *logos* would be especially appropriate, since it includes the idea of a universal essence, and therefore covers the fact that man's clarity of consciousness and capacity for reason are universal rather than something individually unique. Neither is this character of his consciousness personal, but, in the deepest sense, impersonal, and thus in sharp contrast to the *anima*, which is a personal dæmon expressing itself in thoroughly personal moods (therefore animosity !).

In consideration of these psychological facts, I have reserved the term *animus* for women exclusively, because "*mulier non habet animam, sed animum*". Feminine psychology shows an element which is a counterpart to the *anima* of man. It is primarily not of an affective nature, but is a quasi-intellectual element best described by the word "prejudice". The emotional nature of man, not his "mind", corresponds to the conscious nature of woman. Mind makes up the "soul", or better, the "*animus*" of woman, and, just as the *anima* of the man consists of inferior relatedness, full of resentment, so the *animus* of woman consists of inferior judgments, or better said, opinions. (For further details I must refer my reader to my essay cited above, for here I can only mention the general aspects.) The *animus* of the woman consists in a plurality of pre-conceived opinions, and is therefore far less susceptible of personification by one figure, but appears more often as a group or crowd. (A good example of this from parapsychology is the so-called "Imperator"-group in the case of Mrs. Piper.)[1] The *animus*, on a lower level, is an inferior *logos*, a caricature of the differentiated masculine mind, just as the *anima*, on a lower level, is a caricature of the feminine *eros*. Following the parallelism further, we can say that just as *hun* corresponds to *hsing*, translated by Wilhelm as *logos*, so the *eros* of woman corresponds to *ming*, which is translated as fate, *fatum*, destiny, and is interpreted by Wilhelm as *eros*. *Eros* is an interweaving; *logos* is capacity for differentiation, clarifying light; *eros* is relatedness; *logos* is discrimination and detachment. Thus the inferior *logos* in the woman's

[1] Compare Hyslop, *Science and a Future Life*.

animus appears as something quite unrelated, and therefore as an inaccessible prejudice, or as an opinion which, in an irritating way, has nothing to do with the essential nature of the object.

I have often been reproached for personifying the *anima* and *animus* as mythology does, but this reproach would only be justified if it could be proved that in my psychological use of them I concretized these concepts in the mythological way. I must declare once and for all that the personification is not an invention of mine, but is inherent in the nature of the phenomena. It would be unscientific to overlook the fact that the *anima* is a psychic, and therefore personal, partial-system. None of the people who make the charge against me would hesitate a second to say: "I dreamed of Mr. X.," whereas, speaking accurately, he only dreamed of the representation of Mr. X. The *anima* is nothing but a representation of the personal nature of the autonomous partial-system in question. The nature of this partial-system in a transcendental sense, that is to say, beyond the boundaries of experience, we cannot know.

I have defined the *anima* in a man as a personification of the unconscious in general, and have therefore taken it as a bridge to the unconscious, that is, the function of relationship to the unconscious. A statement of our text brings out an interesting connection with this position of mine. The text says that consciousness (that is, personal consciousness), comes from the *anima*. Since the Western mind is based wholly on the standpoint of consciousness, it must define *anima* in the way I have done, but the East, on the contrary, orientated as it is from the view-point of the unconscious, sees consciousness as an effect of the *anima*! Without a doubt, consciousness is derived from the unconscious. This is something we remember too little, and therefore we are always attempting to identify the psyche with consciousness, or at least attempting to represent the unconscious as a derivative, or an effect of the conscious (as, for example, in the Freudian repression theory). But, for the reasons given above, it is essential that nothing be subtracted from the reality of the unconscious, and that the figures of the unconscious should be understood as quantities which produce effects. Whoever has understood the thing meant by psychic reality need not fear falling back into primitive demonology because that reality is admitted. If the unconscious figures are not accorded the dignity of spontaneously effective factors, one becomes the victim of a one-sided belief in the conscious, which finally leads to a state of mental tension. Catastrophes are then bound to occur, because, despite all one's consciousness, the dark psychic powers have been overlooked. It is not we who personify them; they have a personal nature from the very beginning. Only when this is thoroughly recognized can we think of depersonalizing them, or of " overcoming the *anima* ", as our text expresses it.

Here, again, is to be found a great difference between Buddhism and our Western attitude of mind, and again there is a dangerous semblance of agreement. Yoga teaching repudiates all fantasy contents and we do the same, but the East does it on quite different grounds. There, conceptions and teachings prevail which express the creative fantasy in richest measure; in fact, one must protect oneself against the excess of fantasy. We, on the other hand, look upon fantasy as paltry subjective reverie. The figures of the unconscious naturally do not appear as abstract and denuded of all accessories, but, on the contrary, are embedded and interwoven in a web of fantasies of an infinite variety and a bewildering abundance. The East can reject these fantasies because it has long ago sucked the juice from them and stored it in condensed form in formulæ of profound wisdom. But we have never even experienced these fantasies, much less extracted the quintessence from them. We have here to catch up with a large portion of experience, and, only when we have found the sense in apparent nonsense, can we separate the valueless from the valuable. We may rest assured that what we extract from our experiences will be something quite different from what the East offers us to-day. The East came to its knowledge of inner things with a childish ignorance of the world. We, on the other hand, will investigate the psyche and its depths, supported by a tremendously extensive historical and scientific knowledge. At this present moment indeed, knowledge of the external world is the greatest obstacle to introspection, but the psychological need will overcome all obstructions. We are already building up a psychology, a science, that is, which gives us a key to things to which the East found entrance only through abnormal psychic conditions.

THE DETACHMENT OF THE CONSCIOUSNESS FROM THE OBJECT

By understanding the unconscious we free ourselves from its domination. That is the basis and also the aim of the instructions in our text. The pupil is taught how he must concentrate on the Light of the inmost region, and, at the same time, free himself from all outer and inner bondage. His life-will is guided toward a consciousness without content which none the less permits all contents to exist. The *Hui Ming Ching* says about this detachment:—

> "A radiance of Light surrounds the world of the mind.
> We forget each other, quiet and pure, all-powerful and empty.
> Emptiness is lighted up by the radiance of the Heart of Heaven.
> The sea is smooth and mirrors the moon on its surface.
> The clouds vanish in blue space.
> The mountains shine clear.
> Consciousness dissolves itself in vision.
> The disk of the moon floats solitary."

This description of the state of fulfilment pictures a psychic condition which could perhaps best be characterized as a detachment of consciousness from the world, and a withdrawal of it to an extra-mundane point, so to speak. In this way, consciousness is both empty and not empty. It is no longer preoccupied with the images of things but merely contains them. The fullness of the world which heretofore pressed upon it, loses none of its richness and beauty, but no longer rules consciousness. The magical claim of things has ceased because the primordial interweaving of consciousness with the world has finally been disentangled. The unconscious is not projected any more, and so the primal *participation mystique* with things is abolished. Therefore, consciousness is no longer preoccupied with compulsive motives, but becomes vision, as the Chinese text very aptly says.

How did this effect come about ? (We grant at the outset that the Chinese author was first of all not a liar ; secondly, that he was of sound mind ; and, thirdly, that he was even an extraordinarily intelligent man.) To understand or explain the detachment described in the text it is necessary for our minds to take a roundabout way. It cannot be done by mimicry, for nothing would be more childish than to wish to imitate and æstheticize such a condition of the psyche. This detachment is an effect which I know very well from my professional practice ; it is the therapeutic effect *par excellence*, for which I labour with my students and patients ; it aims toward the dissolution of *participation mystique*. With a stroke of genius, Lévy-Brühl [1] has laid down the condition he calls *participation mystique* as the hall-mark of primitive mentality. As described by him it is simply the indefinitely large remnant of non-differentiation between subject and object, which among primitives is still of such proportions that it cannot fail to strike the European consciousness. In so far as the difference between subject and object is not conscious, unconscious identity prevails. Then the unconscious is projected into the object, and the object is introjected into the subject, that is to say, made part of the subjects' psychology. Plants and animals behave like men ; men are at the same time themselves and animals also, and everything is alive with spectres and gods. The civilized man regards himself

[1] *Primitive Mentality.* London: Allen and Unwin.

naturally as immeasurably above these things. None the less, he is often identified with his parents for his whole life, or he is identified with his affects, and shamelessly accuses others of the things he will not see in himself. He too, in a word, has still a remnant of primal unconsciousness, or the state of non-differentiation between subject and object. On account of this unconsciousness, he is magically affected by countless people, things, and circumstances, that is to say, unconditionally influenced. Nearly as much as the primitive, he is beset by disturbing contents and therefore needs just as many apotropæic charms. He no longer works the magic with medicine bags, amulets, and animal sacrifices, but with nerve-remedies, neuroses, "enlightenment," cults of the will, etc.

But if the unconscious can be recognized as a co-determining quantity along with the conscious, and if it can be lived in such a way that conscious and unconscious (in a narrower sense instinctive) demands are given recognition as far as possible, the centre of gravity of the total personality shifts its position. It ceases to be in the ego, which is merely the centre of consciousness, and is located instead, in what might be called a virtual point between the conscious and the unconscious. This new centre might be called the self. If such a transposition succeeds, it results in doing away with *participation mystique*, and there develops a personality who, so to speak, suffers only in the inferior parts of himself, but in the superior regions, to carry out the figure, is singularly detached from painful as well as pleasing events.

The integration and birth of this superior personality is the achievement meant by our text when it speaks of the "holy fruit", the "diamond body", or of any other sort of indestructible body. These expressions are psychologically symbolical of an attitude which is invulnerable to emotional entanglements and violent upheavals; in a word, they symbolize a consciousness freed from the world. I have reasons for believing that this is a natural preparation for death, and sets in after middle life. Death is psychologically just as important as birth and, like this, is an integral part of life. It is not the psychologist who must be questioned as to what happens finally to the detached consciousness. Whatever theoretical position he assumed, he would hopelessly overstep the boundaries of his scientific competence. He can only point out that the views of our text with respect to the timelessness of the detached consciousness, are in harmony with the religious thought of all times and with that of the overwhelming majority of mankind. He can say, further, that anyone who does not think this way would stand outside the human order, and would, therefore, be suffering from a disturbance in his psychic equilibrium. As physician then, I make the greatest effort to fortify, so far as I have the power, a belief in immortality, especially in my older patients to whom such questions come menacingly near. If viewed correctly in the psychological sense, death, indeed, is not an end but a goal, and therefore life for death begins as soon as the meridian is passed.

Chinese yoga philosophy bases itself upon the fact of this instinctive preparation for death as a goal, and, following the analogy with the goal of the first half of life, namely, begetting and reproduction, or the means towards perpetuation of physical life, it takes as the aim of spiritual existence, the begetting and perpetuation of a psychic spirit-body (" subtle body "), which ensures the continuity of the detached consciousness. It is the birth of the pneumatic man, known to the European from antiquity, but which he seeks to produce by quite other symbols and magical practices, by faith and Christian way of life. Here again we stand on a basis quite different from that of the East. Again the text sounds as though it were not very far from Christian ascetic morality, but nothing would be further from the truth than to assume that it is actually dealing with the same thing. Behind our text is a culture thousands of years old, one which has been developed out of, and beyond, primitive instincts, and which, therefore, knows nothing about the brutal morality suited to us as recently civilized, barbaric Teutonic peoples. For this reason, there is lacking to the Chinese that impulse toward violent repression of the instincts which makes our spirituality hysterically exaggerated and poisonous. Whoever lives his instincts can also separate from them, and in just as natural a way as he lived them. Any idea of heroic self-conquest would be entirely foreign to the sense of our text, but it would inevitably amount to that if we followed the Chinese instructions literally.

We must never forget our historical premises. Only a little more than a thousand years ago, we stumbled from the crudest beginnings of polytheism into the midst of a highly developed, oriental religion which lifted the imaginative minds of half-savages to a height which did not correspond to their degree of mental development. In order to keep to this height in some fashion or other, it was unavoidable that the sphere of the instincts should be thoroughly repressed. Therefore, religious practice and morality took on an outspokenly brutal, almost malicious, character. The repressed elements are naturally not developed, but vegetate further in the unconscious and in their original barbarism. We would like to climb the heights of a philosophical religion, but are, in fact, incapable of it. The best we can do is to grow up to it. The Amfortas wound and the Faustian conflict in the Germanic man are not yet healed; his unconscious is still loaded with contents which must first be made conscious before he can be free of them. Recently I received a letter from a former patient which pictures the necessary transformation in simple but expressive words. She writes: " Out of evil, much good has come to me. By keeping quiet, repressing nothing, remaining attentive, and hand in hand with that, by accepting reality—taking things as they are, and not as I wanted them to be—by doing all this, rare knowledge has come to me, and rare powers as well, such as I could never have imagined before. I always thought that, when we accept things, they overpower us in one way or another. Now this is not true at all, and it is only by accepting them that one can define an attitude toward them.[1] So now I intend playing the game of life, being receptive to whatever comes to me, good and bad, sun and shadow that are for ever shifting, and, in this way, also accepting my own nature with its positive and negative sides. Thus everything becomes more alive to me. What a fool I was! How I tried to force everything to go according to my idea!"

Only on the basis of such an attitude, which renounces none of the values won in the course of Christian development, but which, on the contrary, tries with Christian charity and forbearance to accept the humblest things in oneself, will a higher level of consciousness and culture be possible. This attitude is religious in the truest sense, and therefore therapeutic, for all religions are therapies for the sorrows and disorders of the soul. The development of Western intellect and will has lent us the almost devilish

---

[1] Dissolution of *participation mystique*.

capacity for imitating such an attitude, apparently with success too, despite the protests of the unconscious. But it is only a matter of time when the counter position always forces recognition of itself with an even harsher contrast. A more and more unsafe situation comes about by reason of this crass imitation, and, at any time, can be overthrown by the unconscious. A safe foundation is only found when the instinctive premises of the unconscious win the same recognition as the view-points of the conscious. No one will deceive himself as to the fact that this necessary recognition of the unconscious stands in violent opposition to the Western Christian, and especially to the Protestant, cult of consciousness. Despite the fact that the new is always hostile to the old, a deep desire to understand cannot fail to discover that, without the more serious application of our acquired Christian values, the new can never gain ground.

THE FULFILMENT

The growing acquaintanceship with the spiritual East should mean to us only a symbolical expression of the fact that we are entering into connection with the strange elements in ourselves. Denial of our own historical premises would be sheer folly and would be the best way to bring about a second uprooting of consciousness. Only by standing firmly on our own soil can we assimilate the spirit of the East.

Describing people who do not know where the true springs of secret powers lie, the old master, Ku Tê, says: "Worldly people lose the roots and cling to the treetops." The spirit of the East has come out of the yellow earth, and our spirit can, and should, only come out of our own earth. It is for this reason that I approach these problems in a way that has often been criticized as being "psychologism". If "psychology" were meant, I should be flattered, because it is really my purpose to push aside, without mercy, the metaphysical claims of all esoteric teaching. Secret motives of gaining power through words are in ill accord with the profound ignorance which we should have the humility to confess. It is my firm intention to bring into the daylight of psychological understanding, things which have a metaphysical sound, and to do my best to prevent the public from believing in obscure power-words. Let the convinced Christian believe, for that is the duty he has taken upon himself, but the non-Christian has forfeited the grace of faith (perhaps he was cursed from birth in not being able to believe, but only to know). Therefore, he has no right to put his faith elsewhere. To understand metaphysically is impossible; it can only be done psychologically I therefore strip things of their metaphysical wrappings in order to make them objects of psychology. In this way, I can at least get something comprehensible out of them, and can avail myself of it. Moreover, I learn psychological conditions and processes which before were veiled in symbols and out of reach of my understanding. In doing this I am also enabled to follow a path similar to the alleged metaphysical one, and can have similar experiences. Finally, if there should still lurk something metaphysical that cannot be formulated, it would then have the best opportunity of showing itself.

To be specific in this matter, I can say that my admiration for the great Eastern philosophers is as great and as indubitable as my attitude toward their metaphysics is irreverent.[1] I suspect them of being symbolical psychologists, to whom no greater wrong could be done than to be taken literally. If it were really metaphysics that they mean, it would be useless to try to understand them. But if it is psychology, we can not only understand them, but we can profit greatly by them, for then the so-called "metaphysical" comes within the range of experience. If I accept the fact that a god is absolute and beyond all human experience, he leaves me cold. I do not affect him, nor does he affect me. But if I know, on the other hand, that God is a mighty activity in my soul, at once I must concern myself with him; he can then become even unpleasantly important, and in practical ways too, which sounds horribly banal, like everything appearing in the sphere of reality.

The reproach of "psychologism" applies only to a

[1] The Chinese philosophers, in contrast to the dogmatists of the West, are only grateful for such an attitude, because they are masters of their gods also. (R. W.)

fool who thinks he has his soul in his pocket; there are certainly more than enough such fools, because, although we know how to speak big words about the " soul ", the depreciation of psychic things is still a typical Western prejudice. If I make use of the concept "autonomous psychic complex", my public meets it with the ready-made prejudice, " nothing but a psychic complex." Why is one so certain that the soul is " nothing but " ? It is as if we did not know, or else continually forgot, that everything of which we are conscious is an image, and that the psyche is made up of images. The same persons who think that God is depreciated if he is understood to be the thing which is moved, as well as the moving force of the soul, that is an " autonomous complex ", these persons can be so persecuted by uncontrollable affects and neurotic states of mind that their wills and their whole wisdom of life become pitiably inadequate. Has the soul then shown its impotence? Should Master Eckehart also be reproached with " psychologism " when he says: " God must be brought to birth in the soul again and again ? " I think the accusation of " psychologism " can only be cited against an intellect which denies the true nature of the autonomous complex, and seeks to explain it rationally as the result of known facts, that is, as non-existent. This latter judgment is just as arrogant as the " metaphysical " assertion which, overstepping human limitations, entrusts a deity who is outside the range of our experience with the bringing about of our psychic states. " Psychologism " is simply the counterpart of the over-reaching attitude of metaphysics, and just as childish as the latter. But it seems to me far more reasonable to accord the psyche the same validity as is given the empirical world, and to admit that the former has just as much " reality " as the latter. As I see it, the psyche is a world in which the ego is contained. Perhaps there are also fishes who believe that they contain the sea. It is our responsibility to do away with this pervasive illusion if metaphysics is to be approached from the psychological standpoint.

Our text gives us a metaphysical concept of this kind, that is, one which must be understood psychologically; it is the idea of the "diamond body", the indestructible breath-body which develops in the Golden Flower, or in square-inch space.[1] This body is a symbol for a remarkable psychological fact, which, because it is objective, appears at first projected or expressed in forms furnished by the experiences of organic life, that is, as fruit, embryo, child, living body, etc. This fact could best be expressed in the words: It is not I who live, it lives me. The illusion as to the superior powers of the

[1] To a certain extent, our text leaves open the question as to whether by a "continuation of life" a survival after death or a prolongation of physical existence is meant. Expressions such as life-elixir and the like are insidiously obscure. In the later additions it becomes evident that the yoga instructions are understood in a purely physical sense. To a more primitive mind, there is nothing disturbing in this odd mixture of the physical and the spiritual, nor do life and death begin to stand for complete opposites as with us. (Besides the well-known ethnological material, there are the "communications" of the English "rescue circles" which, with their thoroughly archaic ideas, are particularly interesting in this connection.) The same ambiguity about immortality is also present in early Christianity where it depends on quite similar assumptions, that is, on the idea of a "breath-body", the essential carrier of life. Geley's para-psychological theory would be the latest reincarnation of this ancient idea. But since we have in our text, also, warnings against the application of the idea in a superstitious way (for example, the superstition about making gold), we can confidently insist on the spiritual meaning of the text. In the conditions which the instructions seek to produce, the physical body plays an increasingly inessential role because of being replaced by the "spirit body" (therefore, the importance of breathing in yoga practice in general). The "breath-body" is not "spiritual" in our sense. It is characteristic of the Westerner that, for purposes of knowledge, he has split apart the physical and the spiritual sides of life, but these opposites lie together in the psyche, and psychology must recognize the fact. The "psychic" is both physical and mental. The ideas in our text all have to do with this "intermediate" world which seems unclear and confused to us because the concept of psychic reality is not yet current among us, although it expresses the actual sphere of life. Without the psyche, mind is as dead as matter, because both are artificial abstractions; to primordial intuitions, however, mind is a volatile body, and matter is not lacking in soul.

conscious leads to the belief : I live. If, by the recognition of the unconscious, this illusion is shattered, the unconscious appears as something objective of which the ego is a part. The attitude toward the unconscious is then analogous to the feeling of a primitive man to whom a son guarantees continuation of life. This is a thoroughly characteristic feeling which can even assume grotesque forms as in the case of the old negro, who, in a rage, called out to his disobedient son : " There he stands, with my body, if you please, but does not even obey me ! "

The fact that the unconscious is looked upon as something in which the ego is contained, brings about a change in inner feeling similar to that experienced by a father to whom a son has been born, a change known to us through the confession of the Apostle Paul : " No longer do I live, but Christ liveth in me." The symbol " Christus " as the " son of man " leads to an analogous psychic experience. It is as if a higher spiritual being of human form were invisibly born in the individual as a spiritual body which is to serve us as a future dwelling, a body which, as Paul expresses himself, is put on like a garment (" Ye who have put on Christ "). Obviously it is always an unfortunate thing to express, in intellectual terms, subtle feelings which are none the less infinitely important for the life and well-being of the individual. In a certain sense, the thing we are trying to express is the feeling of having been " replaced ", but without the connotation of having been " deposed ". It is as if the leadership of the affairs of life had gone over to an invisible centre. Nietzsche's metaphor, "In most loving bondage, free,"[1] would be appropriate here. Religious speech is full of imaginative expressions that picture this feeling of free dependence, of calm and devotion.

[1] "*Frei in liebevollstem Muss.*"

In this remarkable experience I see a phenomenon resulting from the detachment of consciousness, through which the subjective " I live ", becomes the objective " It lives me ". This condition is felt to be higher than the earlier one; it is really as if it were a sort of release from compulsion and impossible responsibility which are the inevitable results of *participation mystique*. This feeling of release filled Paul completely. It is the consciousness of being a child of God which then frees one from the spell of the blood. Also, it is a feeling of reconciliation with what is happening, and that is the reason that the glance of " one who has attained fulfilment ", according to the *Hui Ming Ching*, returns to the beauty of nature.

In the Pauline Christ-symbol the deepest religious experience of the West and East meet. On the one hand, Christ the sorrow-laden hero; on the other, the Golden Flower that blooms in the purple hall of the city of jade—what a contrast, what an unfathomable difference, what an abyss of history ! This is a problem fit to be the master-work of a future psychologist.

Among the so-called great religious problems of the present, there is to be found one which, from the attention accorded it, might be assumed to be quite a small one, but which, in fact, is the main problem of our day, namely, the problem of the progress of religious spirit.[1] If that is discussed, it is necessary to emphasize the difference between the East and the West in their treatment of the " jewel ", that is, the central symbol. The West emphasizes the becoming human, and even the personality and historicity of Christ, while the East says : " Without beginning, without end, without past, without future." [2] Following his conception, the Christian subordinates

[1] For the sake of clarity of meaning the author has amplified the above sentence for this edition. (C. F. B.)
[2] *Hui Ming Ching*, p. 108.

himself to the superior, divine person in expectation of his grace; but the Eastern man knows that redemption depends on the " works " a person devotes to himself. Out of the individual grows the whole *Tao*. The *Imitatio Christi* will for ever have this disadvantage: we worship a man as a divine model embodying the deepest meaning of life, and then, out of sheer imitation, we forget to make real the profound meaning present in ourselves. As a matter of fact, it is not altogether uncomfortable to renounce one's real meaning. If Jesus had done that, he would have become a respectable carpenter, and not the religious rebel, to whom the same thing would happen to-day as happened then.

Imitation of Christ can easily be understood in a deeper way. It can be taken as the duty to put into reality one's best conviction, always the completest expression of individual temperament, with the same courage and self-sacrifice shown by Jesus. Happily not everyone has the task of being a leader of humanity, or a great rebel; and so, after all, it is quite possible for each to realize himself in his own way. Perfect honesty might even become an ideal. Since great innovations always begin in the most improbable places, the fact, for example, that a man is not nearly as ashamed of his nakedness as he used to be, might be the beginning of a recognition of himself as he is. Hard upon this will follow the recognition of many other things that are now strictly taboo, because the reality of the earth will not for ever remain veiled like the *virgines velandæ* of Tertullian. Moral unmasking is only one step further in the same direction, and behold, there stands a man as he is, and confesses himself to be as he is. If he does this in a meaningless way, he is a chaotic fool, but if he knows the significance of what he does, he can belong to a higher order of man who, regardless of suffering, makes real the Christ symbol. It can often be observed, that wholly concrete taboos or magical rites in an early stage of a religion, become in the next stage, a matter of concern to the soul, or even purely spiritual symbols. An external law can, in the course of development, become an inner conviction. Thus it could easily happen to the Protestant that the person Jesus, now removed by centuries, could become the superior man within himself. There would then be reached in a European way, the psychological condition corresponding to that of the " enlightened one " in the Eastern sense.

All this is a step in the developmental process of a higher human consciousness that finds itself on the way toward unknown goals ; it is not metaphysics in the ordinary sense. In the first place, and thus far, it is only " psychology ", but also thus far it can be experienced, it is intelligible, and—thank God—it is real, a reality with which something can be done, a reality containing possibilities and therefore alive. The fact that I restrict myself to what can be psychically experienced, and repudiate the metaphysical, does not mean, as anyone with insight can understand, a gesture of scepticism or agnosticism pointed against faith or trust in higher powers, but what I intend to say is approximately the same thing Kant meant when he called " *das Ding an sich* " (the thing in itself), a " purely negative, borderline " concept. Every statement about the transcendental ought to be avoided because it is invariably a laughable presumption on the part of the human mind, unconscious of its limitations. Therefore, when God or *Tao* is spoken of as a stirring of, or a condition of, the soul, something has been said about the knowable only, but nothing about the unknowable. Of the latter, nothing can be determined.

CONCLUSION

The aim of my commentary is the effort to build a bridge of psychological understanding between East and West. The basis of every real understanding is man, and therefore I had to speak of human things. That must excuse me for having dealt only with the general aspects, and for not having entered into what is specifically technical. Technical instructions are valuable for those who know for example, what a photographic apparatus or a motor is, but they are useless for anyone who has no idea of such apparatus. Yet the Western man for whom I write finds himself in this situation, that is, ignorant of his own apparatus. Therefore it seemed above all important to me, to emphasize the agreement between the psychic conditions and the symbolism of East and West, because, by means of these analogies, there is opened a way to the inner chambers of the Eastern mind. This way does not demand the sacrifice of our own nature and does not threaten us with being torn from our roots. Furthermore, it is not an intellectual telescope, or microscope, offering a view which at bottom does not concern us because it does not grip us. It is rather the atmosphere of suffering, seeking, and striving common to all civilized peoples; it is the tremendous experiment of becoming conscious, which nature has imposed on mankind, uniting the most diverse cultures in a common task.

Western consciousness is by no means consciousness in general, but rather a historically conditioned, and geographically limited, factor, representative of only one part of humanity. The widening of our own consciousness ought not to proceed at the expense of other kinds of consciousness, but ought to take place through the development of those elements of our psyche which are analogous to those of a foreign psyche, just as the East cannot do without our technique, science, and industry. The European invasion of the East was a deed of violence on a great scale, and it has left us the duty—*noblesse oblige*—of understanding the mind of the East. This is perhaps more necessary than we realize at present.

EXAMPLES OF EUROPEAN *MANDALAS*

These pictures have been made in the way described in the text, by patients during the course of treatment. The earliest picture dates from 1916. All the pictures have been done independently of any Eastern influence. The *I Ching* hexagrams in picture No. 4 come from the reading of Legge's translation in the *Sacred Books of the East* series but they were only put into the picture because their content seemed, to the academically educated patient, especially meaningful in her life. No European *maṇḍalas* known to me (I have a fairly large collection), achieve the conventionally and traditionally established harmony and completeness of the Eastern *maṇḍala*. Therefore, from the infinite variety of European *maṇḍalas*, I have made a choice of ten pictures, which, at least when taken as a whole, ought to illustrate clearly the parallelism between Eastern philosophy and unconscious European ideas in their formative state.

C. G. JUNG.

DESCRIPTION OF THE PLATES

1. ♀ The Golden Flower represented as the most splendid of all flowers.

2. ♀ In the centre, the Golden Flower; radiating out from it, fishes as fertility symbols (corresponding to the thunderbolts of the *lamaist maṇḍalas*).

3. ♂ A luminous flower in the centre, with stars rotating about it. Around the flower, walls with eight gates. The whole conceived as a transparent window.

4. ♀ Separation of the air and earth. (Birds and serpents.) In the centre a flower with a golden star.

5. ♀ Separation of the light, from the dark world; the divine from the earhtly soul. In the centre a representation of contemplation.

6. ♂ In the centre, the white light shining in the firmament; in the first circle, protoplasmic life-seeds; in the second, rotating cosmic principles which contain the four fundamental colours; in the third and fourth, a creative force working inward and outward. At the cardinal points, the masculine and feminine souls, both again divided into light and dark.

7. ♀ Representation of *tetraktys* in rotating movement.

8. ♀ The child in the germinal vesicle with the four fundamental colours included in the circular movement.

9. ♀ In the centre, the germinal vesicle with human figure nourished by blood vessels which have their origin in the cosmos. The cosmos rotates around the centre which attracts its emanations. Around the outside is spread nervous tissue indicating that the process is going on in the *solar plexus*.

10. ♂ A *maṇḍala* as a fortified city with walls and moats. Within, a broad moat surrounded by a wall, fortified with sixteen towers and another moat following this wall. The last moat surrounds a central castle with golden roofs whose centre is a golden temple.

I

2

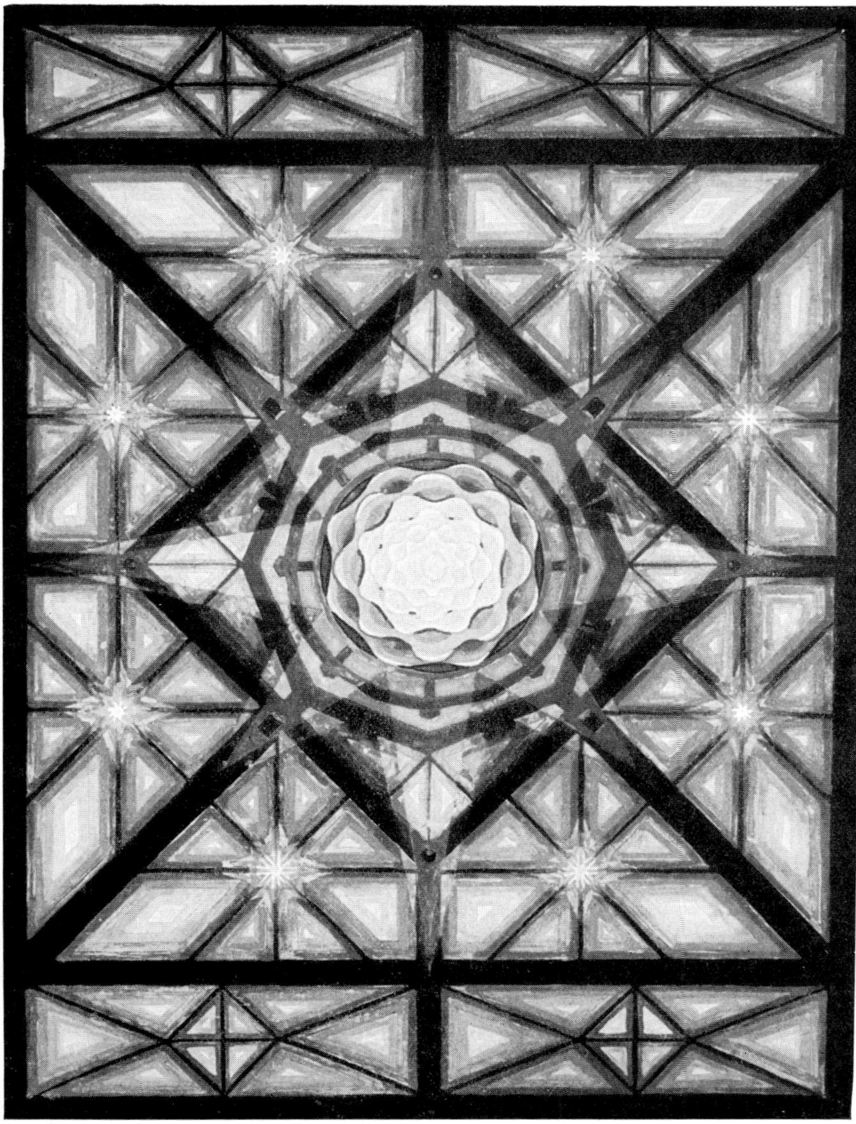

3

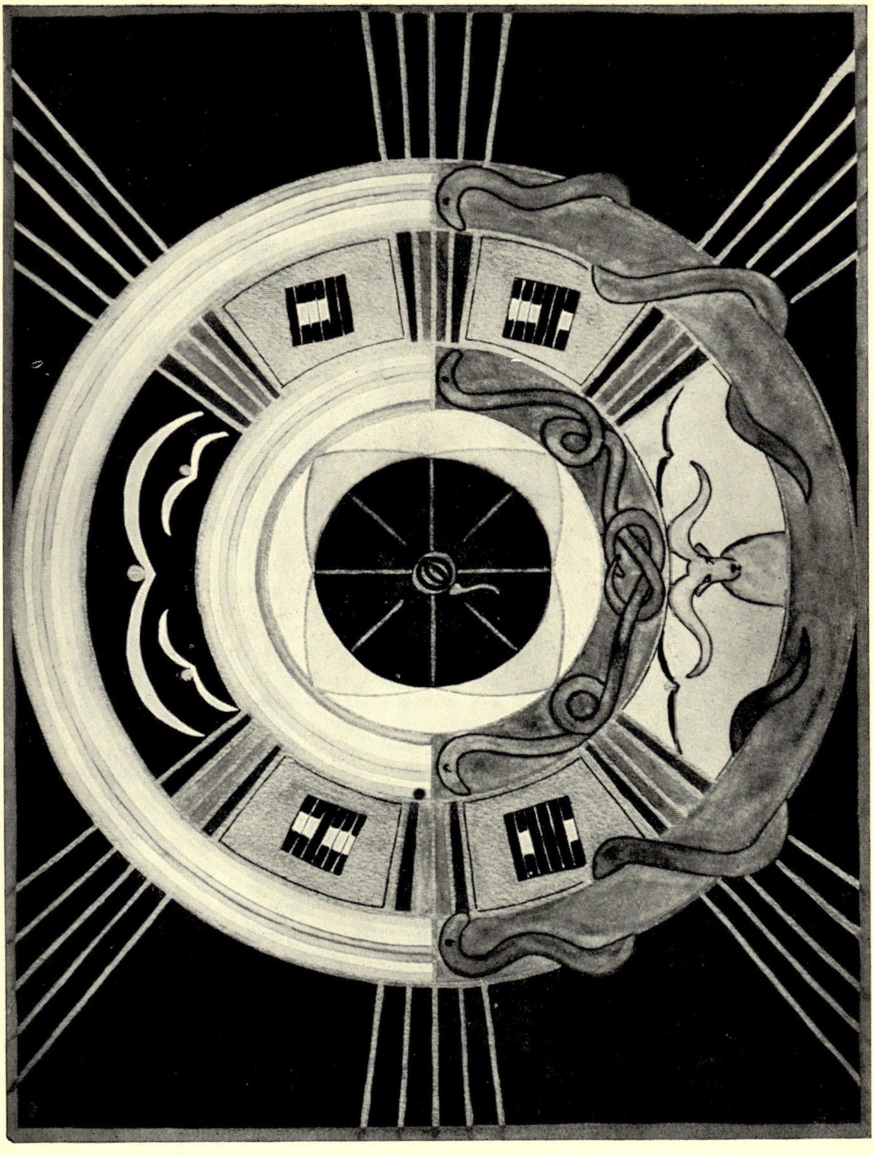

4

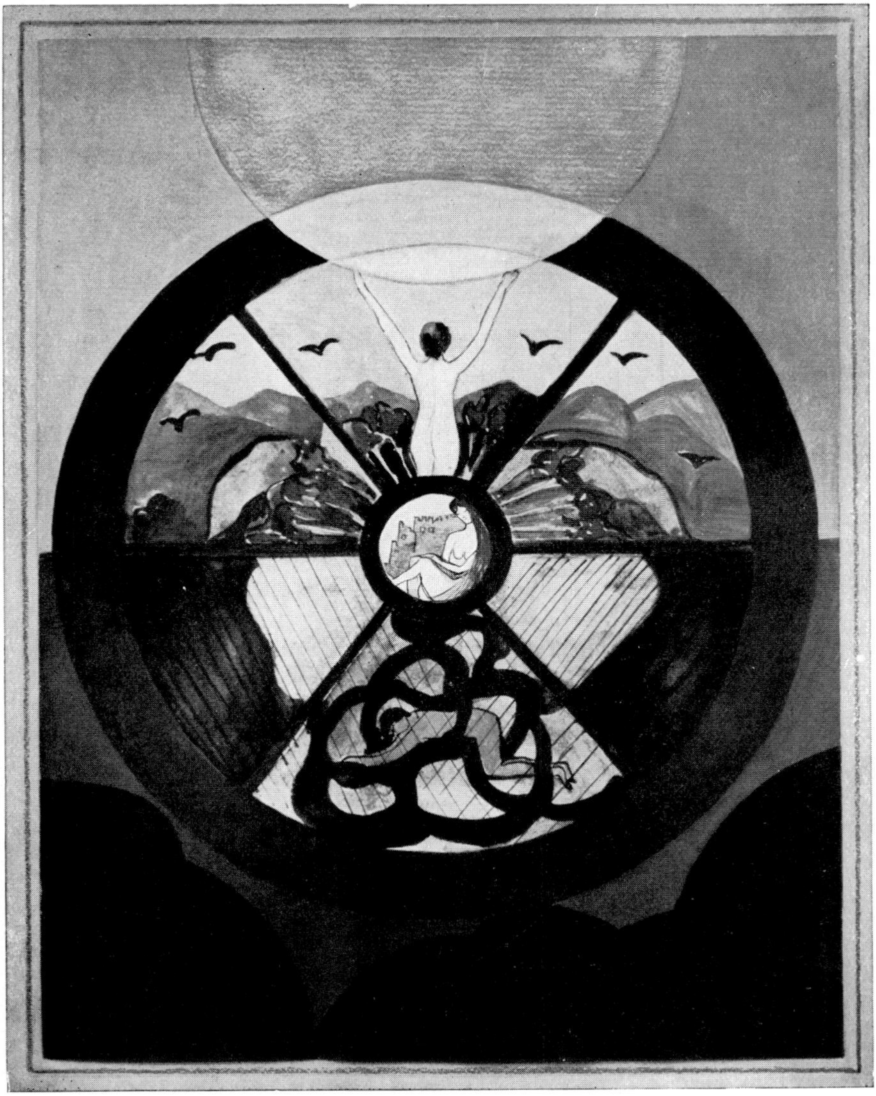

6

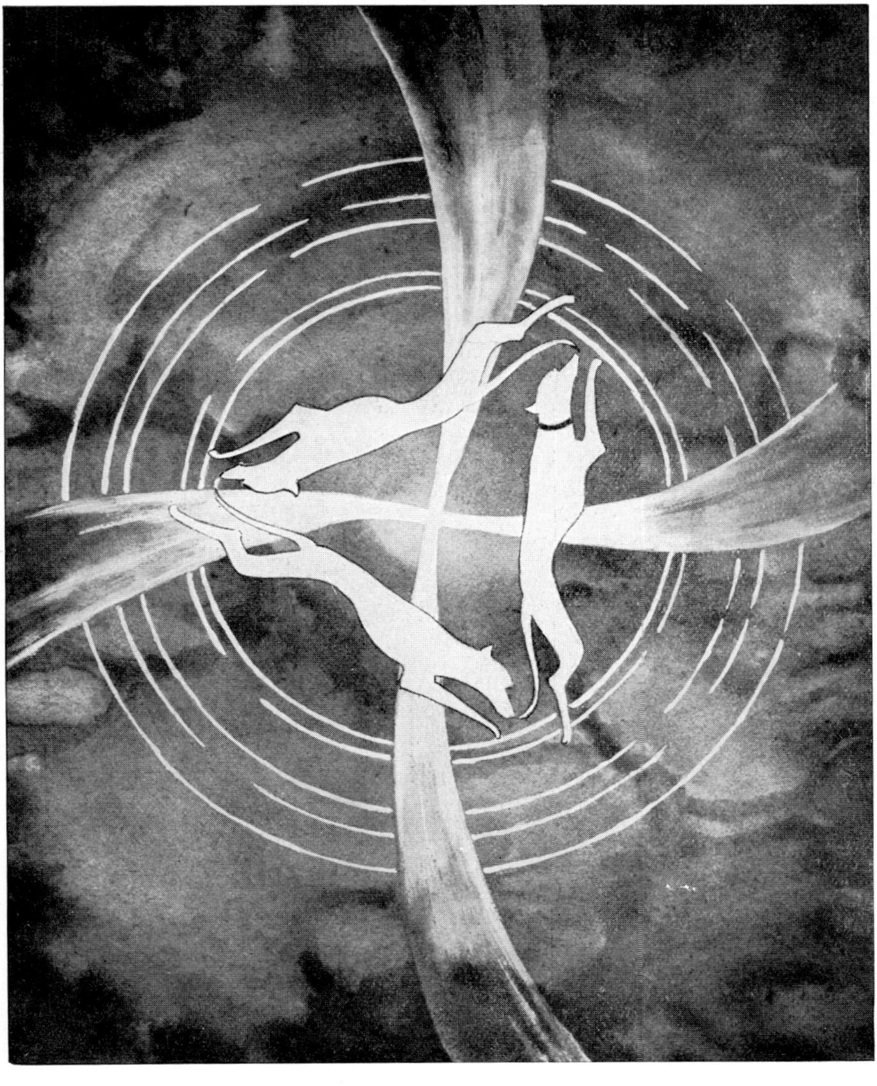

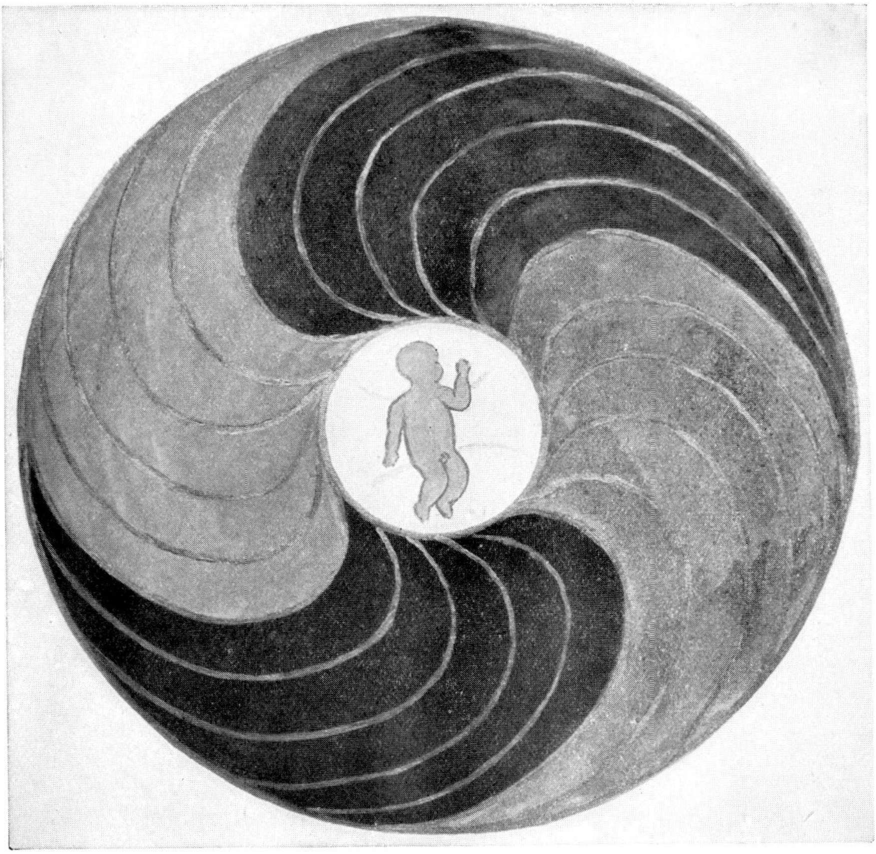

8

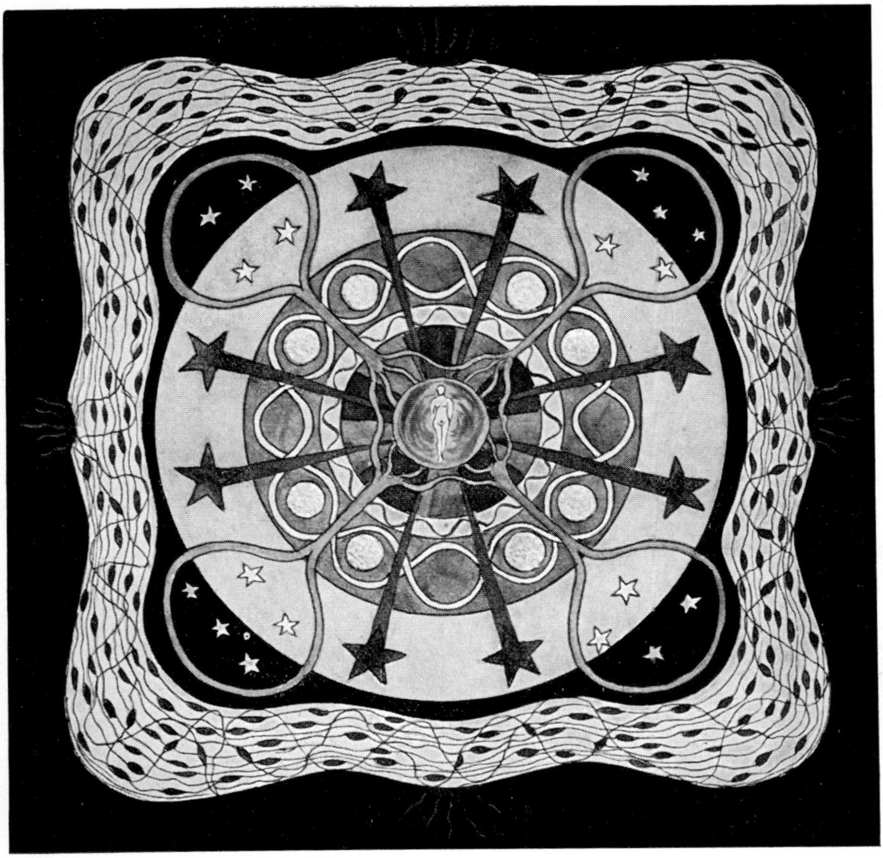

9

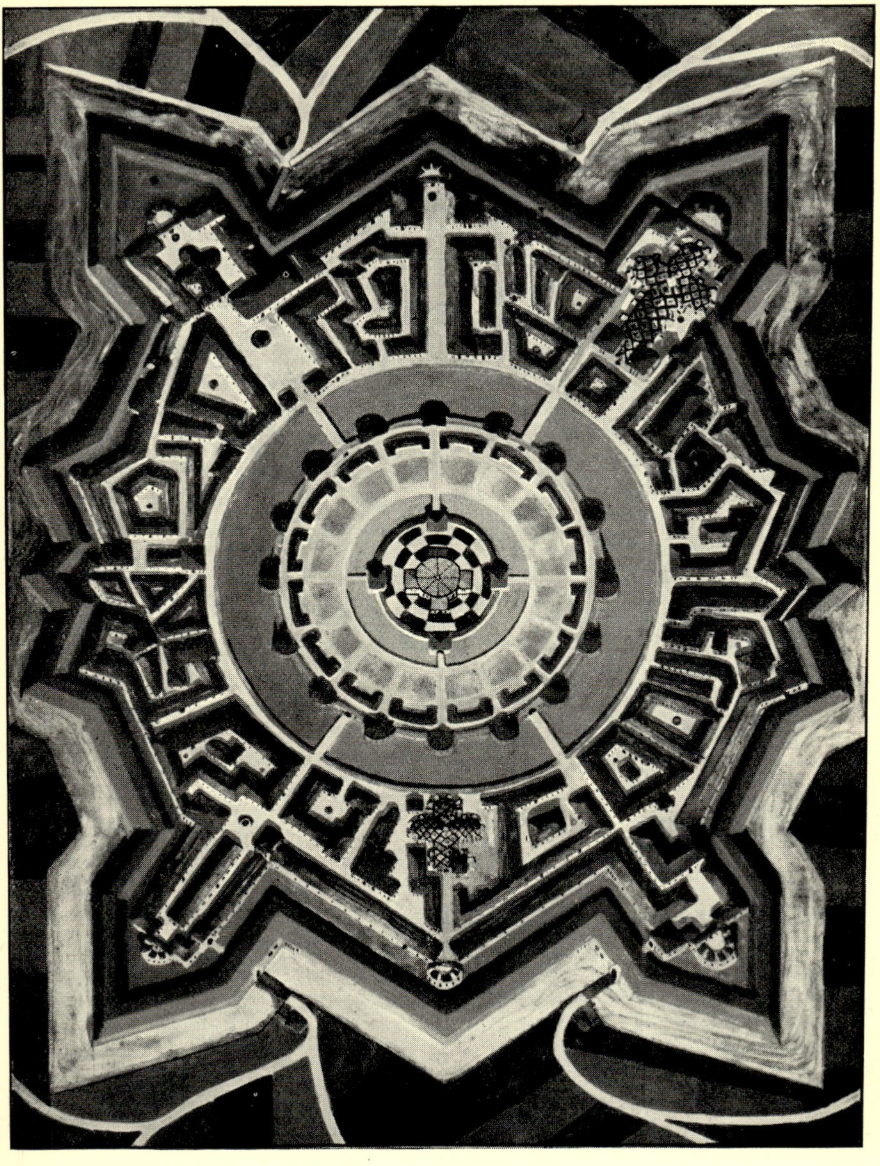

APPENDIX

In Memory of Richard Wilhelm [1]

By C. G. Jung

It is no easy task for me to speak of Richard Wilhelm and his work, because, starting very far away from one another, our ways crossed in a comet-like fashion. You probably knew Wilhelm before I became acquainted with him, and his life-work has a range which I have not encompassed. Nor have I seen the China that first shaped and later continued to engross him, nor am I familiar with its language, the living spiritual expression of the Chinese East. I stand, indeed, as a stranger outside that vast territory of knowledge and experience in which Wilhelm worked as a master of his profession. He as a sinologue, and I a physician, should never have come into contact with one another had we remained specialists. But we met in a field of humanity which begins beyond academic boundary posts. There lay our point of contact; there the spark leaped across that kindled the light which was to become for me, one of the most meaningful events of my life. Because of this experience I may speak of Wilhelm and his work, thinking with grateful reverence of this mind which created a bridge between East and West and gave to the Occident the heirship to a precious culture thousands of years old, a culture perhaps destined to disappear.

Wilhelm possessed the mastership which is only

[1] This memorial address was delivered in Munich, May 10th, 1930.

won by the man who surmounts his speciality, and so his science became a concern touching all humanity— I must not say became—it was that at the beginning and remained so always. For what else could have freed him from the narrow horizons of the European, of the missionary, in fact, so that no sooner had he encountered the secret of the Chinese soul than he perceived the treasure hidden there for us, and sacrificed his European prejudice on behalf of this rare pearl? It could only have been an all-embracing humanness, a greatness of heart that divines the whole, which enabled him to open himself without reservation to a profoundly foreign spirit, and to put at the service of this influence the manifold gifts and capacities of his mind. Reaching beyond all Christian *resentiment*, beyond all European presumption, his comprehending devotion is in itself witness of a rarely great spirit, whereas all mediocre minds in contact with a foreign culture either lose themselves in blind self-deracination, or in an equally uncomprehending, as well as presumptuous, passion for criticism. Touching only the superficialities and externals of the foreign culture, they never eat its bread nor drink its wine, and so never enter into the *communio spiritus*, that most intimate transfusion and interpenetration which prepares a new birth.

As a rule, the specialist's is a purely masculine mind, an intellect to which fertilization is a foreign and unnatural process, therefore it is an especially ill-adapted tool for receiving and bringing to birth a foreign spirit. But a greater mind bears the stamp of the feminine, and is given a receptive and fruitful womb which can re-shape what is strange into a familiar form. Wilhelm possessed in the highest degree the rare *charisma* of spiritual motherhood. To it he owed his unequalled ability to feel his way into the spirit of the East, which made possible his incomparable translations.

To me, the greatest of his achievements is the translation of, and commentary on, the *I Ching*. Before I learned to know Wilhelm's translation, I had for years worked with Legge's inadequate translation, and was therefore in a position to recognize fully the extraordinary difference. Wilhelm has succeeded in bringing to life again in a new and vital form, this ancient work in which not only many sinologues, but even many modern Chinese as well, can see nothing but a collection of absurd magical formulæ. This work embodies, as perhaps no other, the spirit of Chinese culture. The best minds of China have collaborated upon it and contributed to it for thousands of years. Despite its fabulous age, it has never grown old, but lives and operates still, at least for those who understand its meaning. That we too belong to this favoured group, we owe to the creative efforts of Wilhelm. He has brought this work close to us, not only through careful translation, but also through his personal experience, on the one hand, as a pupil of a Chinese master of the old school, on the other, as an initiate in the psychology of Chinese yoga, to whom the practical application of the *I Ching* was an ever-renewed experience.

But with these rich gifts, Wilhelm has also bequeathed us a task whose magnitude we may, at the present time, suspect, but certainly cannot fathom. Anyone like myself, who has had the rare good fortune to experience in a spiritual exchange with Wilhelm, the divinatory power of the *I Ching*, cannot for long remain ignorant of the fact that we have touched here an Archimedean point from which our Western attitude of mind can be shaken to its foundations. Truly it is no small service to have produced for us, as Wilhelm did, such an inclusive and richly-coloured painting of a foreign culture, but it will be almost nothing in comparison with the fact that, over and beyond this, he has infected us with a living germ of the Chinese spirit, which is capable of making an essential change in our world picture. We have not remained merely admiring or critical observers, but have become participants of the Eastern spirit in so far as we have succeeded in experiencing the living potency of the *I Ching*.

The function on which the use of the *I Ching* is based, if I may so express myself, is apparently in sharp contradiction to our Western, scientifically-causal, *Weltanschauung*. In other words, it is extremely unscientific, taboo in fact, and therefore out of reach of our scientific judgment, and incomprehensible to it.

Some years ago, the then president of the British Anthropological Society asked me how I could explain the fact that so highly intellectual a people as the Chinese had produced no science. I replied that this must really be an " optical illusion ", because the Chinese did have a science whose " standard work " was the *I Ching*, but that the principle of this science, like so much else in China, was altogether different from our scientific principle.

The science of the *I Ching* is not based on the causality principle, but on a principle (hitherto unnamed because not met with among us) which I have tentatively called the *synchronistic* principle. My occupation with the psychology of unconscious processes long ago necessitated my looking about for another principle of explanation, because the causality principle seemed to me inadequate to explain certain remarkable phenomena of the psychology of the unconscious. Thus I found that there are psychic parallelisms which cannot be related to each other causally, but which must be connected through another sequence of events. This connection seemed to me to be essentially provided in the fact of the relative simultaneity, therefore the expression "synchronistic". It seems indeed, as though time, far from being an abstraction, is a concrete continuum which contains qualities or basic conditions manifesting themselves simultaneously in various places in a way not to be explained by causal parallelisms, as, for example, in cases of the coincident appearance of identical thoughts, symbols, or psychic conditions. Another example would be the simultaneity of Chinese and European periods of style, a fact pointed out by Wilhelm. They could never have been causally related to one another. Astrology would be a large scale example of synchronism, if it had at its disposal thoroughly tested findings. But at least there are some facts adequately tested and fortified by a wealth of statistics which make the astrological problem seem worthy of philosophical investigation. (It is assured of recognition from psychology, without further restrictions, because astrology represents the summation of all the psychological knowledge of antiquity.)

The fact that it is possible to construct, in adequate fashion, a person's character from the data of his nativity, shows the relative validity of astrology. But the birth never depends on the actual astronomical constellations, but upon an arbitrary, purely conceptual time-system, because by reason of the precession of the equinoxes, the spring point has long ago passed on beyond zero degree Aries. In so far as there are any really correct astrological deductions, they are not due to the effects of the constellations, but to our hypothetical time-characters. In other words, whatever is born or done this moment of time, has the qualities of this moment of time.

This is also the fundamental formula for the use of the *I Ching*. As is known, one gains knowledge of the hexagram characterizing the moment by a method of manipulating sticks of yarrow, or coins, a method depending on purest chance. As the moment is, so do the runic sticks fall. The only question is: Did the old King Wên, and the Duke of Chou, in the year 1000 B.C., interpret the accidental picture made by the fallen runic sticks correctly or not? As to this, experience alone can decide.

At his first lecture at the Psychological Club in Zürich, Wilhelm, at my request, demonstrated the method of consulting the *I Ching*, and, at the same time, made a prognosis, which, in less than two years, was fulfilled to the letter and with unmistakable clearness. This fact could be further confirmed by many parallel experiences. However, I am not concerned with establishing objectively the validity of the prophecies of the *I Ching*, but take it as a premise, just as my deceased friend did. Therefore, I am only going to discuss the amazing fact that the *qualitas occulta* of the time-moment became legible by means of the hexagram of the I *Ching*. One is dealing with a relationship of events, not only analogous to astrology, but essentially related to it. The birth corresponds to the sticks that are thrown, the constellation to the hexagram, and the astrological interpretation arising from the constellation corresponds to the text appropriate to the hexagram.

The type of thought built on the synchronistic principle, which reaches its high point in the *I Ching*, is the purest expression of Chinese thinking in general. With us, this thinking has been absent from the history of philosophy since the time of Heraclitus, and only reappears as a faint echo in Leibnitz. However, in the time between, it was not extinguished, but continued to live in the twilight of astrological speculation, and remains to-day at this level.

At this point the *I Ching* touches the need of further development in us. Occultism has enjoyed in our times a renaissance which is really without a parallel. The light of the Western mind is nearly darkened by it. I am not thinking now of our seats of learning and their representatives. I am a physician and deal with ordinary people, and therefore I know that the universities have ceased to act as disseminators of light. People have become weary of scientific specialization and rationalistic intellectualism. They want to hear truths which do not make them narrower but broader, which do not obscure but enlighten, which do not run off them like water, but pierce them to the marrow. This search threatens to lead a large, if anonymous, public into wrong paths.

When I think of Wilhelm's achievement and significance, I am reminded of Anquetil du Perron, the Frenchman who brought the first translation of the Upanishads to Europe just at the period when, for the first time in almost 1,800 years, something unheard-of occurred, and the goddess of reason drove the Christian Godhead from the throne in Nôtre Dame. To-day, when, in Russia, there occur things far more unheard-of than at that time in Paris, when, in Europe itself, the Christian symbol has reached such a condition of feebleness that even the Buddhists think the right moment has come for a mission in Europe, it is Wilhelm, who, as though chosen from the soul of Europe, brings us a new light from the East. This is the cultural task to which Wilhelm felt himself called. He recognized how much the East could give toward the healing of our spiritual need.

A beggar is not helped by our giving him outright more or less generous alms, although he may desire it.

He is much better helped if we show him the way to free himself permanently of his need by work. Unfortunately, the spiritual beggars of our time are all too inclined to accept the alms of the East in specie, that is, to appropriate unthinkingly the spiritual possessions of the East and to imitate its way blindly. That is the danger about which it is impossible to give too many warnings, and the one which Wilhelm also felt very clearly. Spiritual Europe is not helped by what is merely a new sensation or a new titillation to the nerves. What it has taken China thousands of years to build cannot be stolen by us. We must learn to acquire it in order to possess it. What the East has to give us should be merely a help in a work which we still have to do. Of what use to us is the wisdom of the Upanishads or the insight of the Chinese yoga, if we desert the foundations of our own culture as though they were outlived errors, and, like homeless pirates, settle with thievish intent on foreign shores? The insight of the East, above all, the wisdom of the *I Ching*, has no meaning when we close our minds to our own problems, when we lead artificially arranged lives on the basis of conventional prejudices, when we veil from ourselves our real human nature with all its dangerous, subterranean elements, and its darkness? The light of this wisdom only shines in the dark, not in the electric searchlight of the European theatre of consciousness and will. The wisdom of the *I Ching*, has originated from a background, whose horror we can faintly suspect if we read of Chinese massacres, of the sinister power of Chinese secret societies, of the nameless poverty, the hopeless filth and vices, of the Chinese masses.

We need to have a correctly three dimensional life if we wish to experience Chinese wisdom as a living thing. Therefore, we first have need of European truths about ourselves. Our way begins in European reality and not in yoga practices which would only serve to lead us astray as to our own reality. We must continue Wilhelm's work of translation in a wider sense if we wish to show ourselves worthy pupils of the master. Just as he translated the spiritual treasure of the East into European meaning, we should translate this meaning into life.

As you know, Wilhelm translated the central concept of *Tao* by Meaning. To translate Meaning into life, that is, to realize *Tao*, would be the task of the pupil. But *Tao* will never be created with words and good precepts. Do we know exactly how *Tao* develops in us or around us? Is it by imitation, or by reason, or by acrobatics of the will? We feel that all these things are ridiculously incommensurate with the task. But where shall we begin with this task? Will Wilhelm's spirit be in us or with us if we do not solve this problem in a truly European way, that is in reality? Or must this be at the last only a rhetorical question whose answer is lost in applause?

Let us look toward the East : there an overwhelming fate is fulfilling itself. European cannon have burst open the gates of Asia; European science and technique, European worldly-mindedness and cupidity, flood China. We have conquered the East politically. Do you know what happened when Rome overthrew the near-East politically? The spirit of the East entered Rome. Mithra became the Roman military god, and out of the most unlikely corners of Asia Minor, came a new spiritual Rome. Would it be unthinkable that the same thing might happen to-day and find us just as blind as were the cultured Romans who marvelled at the superstitions of the *Christoi*? It is to be noted that England and Holland, the two main colonizing powers in Asia, are also the two most infected with theosophy. I know that our unconscious is full of Eastern symbolism. The spirit of the East is really before our gates. Therefore it seems to me that the realization of the Meaning, the search for *Tao*, has already become a collective phenomenon among us, and that to a far greater extent than we generally think. For example I take, as a very important sign of the times, the fact that Wilhelm and the indologue Hauer, were asked to lecture on yoga at this year's congress of German psychotherapists. Let us realize what it means for a practical physician who deals directly with a suffering, and therefore receptive, person, to send out a feeler toward an Eastern therapeutic system! Thus the spirit of the East penetrates through all our pores and reaches the most vulnerable places of Europe. It could be a dangerous infection, but perhaps it is also a remedy. The Babylonian confusion of tongues in the Western world has created such a disorientation that everyone longs for simpler truths, or at least for general ideas which speak, not to the head alone, but to the heart as well, which give clarity to the spirit, and peace to the restless pressure of the feelings. Like the ancient Romans, we again to-day, are importing every form of exotic superstition in the hope of discovering therein the right cure for our disease.

Human instinct knows that all great truth is simple, and therefore the man who is weak in instinct assumes great truth to exist in all cheap simplifications and platitudes. Or, as a result of his disappointment, he falls into the opposite error of thinking that great truth must be as obscure and complicated as possible. We have to-day a gnostic movement in the anonymous masses, which exactly corresponds psychologically with the movement 1,900 years ago. Then, as to-day, lonely wanderers like the great Apollonius, spun the spiritual threads from Europe back to Asia, perhaps to remotest India.

Looked at from such a historical perspective, I see Wilhelm in the guise of one of those great gnostic intermediaries who brought the cultural heritage of Asia into contact with the Hellenic spirit, and thereby caused a new world to rise out of the ruins of the Roman Empire. Then, as now, insipidity, inflated ideas, bad taste, and inner unrest prevailed. Then, as now, the continent of the spirit was inundated, leaving only single peaks projecting like so many islands from the vague flood. Then, as now, all sorts of devious paths beckoned the spirit and the wheat of false prophets bloomed.

In the midst of the clanging disharmony of the concert of European opinion, to hear the simple language of Wilhelm, the messenger from China, is a real blessing. One can see from it that it has been schooled in the plant-like naïveté of the Chinese mind, which is able to express profound things in simple language; it discloses something of the simplicity of great truth, the ingenuousness of deep meaning, and it carries to us the delicate perfume of the Golden Flower. Penetrating gently, it has set in the soil of Europe a tender seedling, for us a new presentment of life and Meaning, after all the spasm of arbitrariness and presumption.

Towards the foreign culture of the East, Wilhelm displayed an extraordinarily large amount of modesty, something unusual in a European. He erected no barrier against it, no prejudices, no assumptions of knowing better, but instead, opened heart and mind to it. He let himself be gripped and shaped by it, so that when he came back to Europe, he brought us not only in his spirit, but also in his nature, a true image of the East. This deep transformation was certainly not won by him without great sacrifice, because our historical premises are so entirely different from those of the East. The keenness of Western consciousness and its glaring problems had to soften before the more universal, more equable nature of the East, and Western rationalism with its one-sided differentiation had to yield to Eastern breadth and simplicity. To Wilhelm, these changes certainly meant not only a shifting of intellectual standpoint, but also an essential rearrangement of the component parts of his personality. The picture of the East he has given us, free as it was from ulterior motive and any trace of violence, could never have been created in such completeness by Wilhelm, had he not been able to let the European in himself slip into the background. If he had allowed East and West to clash against each other within him with an unyielding harshness, he could not have fulfilled his mission of providing us with a true picture of China.

Wilhelm fulfilled his mission in every sense of the word. Not only did he make accessible to us the dead treasures of the Chinese mind, but, as I have pointed out, he brought with him its spiritual root, the root that has lived all these thousands of years, and planted it in the soil of Europe. With the completion of his task, his mission reached its climax, and, unfortunately, its end also. According to the law of *enantiodromia*, so clearly understood by the Chinese, there grew out of the close of the one phase the beginning of its opposite. Thus, in its culmination, *yang* goes over into *yin*, and position is resolved into negation. I came near to Wilhelm only in the last years of his life, and then I could observe how, with the completion of his life-work, Europe and the European man drew closer and closer to him, beset him in fact. At the same time, there developed in him the feeling that he might be standing on the brink of a great change, a transformation whose nature it is true he could not clearly grasp. He only knew that he was faced with a decisive crisis. His physical illness went parallel with this spiritual development. His dreams were filled with Chinese memories, but they were always sad and dismal pictures that hovered before him, a clear proof that the Chinese contents had become negative.

There is nothing that can be sacrificed for ever. Everything returns later in a changed form, and where so great a sacrifice has once taken place, when the sacrificed thing returns, there must be ready a healthy and resistant body in order to be able to meet the shock of a great transformation. Therefore, a spiritual crisis of such dimensions often means death if it takes place in a body weakened by disease. For now the sacrificial knife is in the hand of him who has been sacrificed, and a death is demanded of him who was once the sacrificer.

As you see, I have not withheld my personal ideas, because if I had not told how I experienced Wilhelm, how else would it have been possible for me to speak of him? Wilhelm's life-work is of so great a value to me because it explains and confirms so much of what I had been seeking, striving for, thinking, and doing, in order to meet the psychic ills of Europe. It was a tremendous experience for me to hear through him in clear language, the things that had been dimly shadowed forth to me from out of the confusion of the European unconscious. As a matter of fact, I feel myself so very much enriched by him that it seems to me as if I had received more from him than from any other man, and this is the reason I do not feel it a presumption if I am the one to offer, on the altar of his memory, the gratitude and respect of all of us.

299.5 a
T 12

**DO NOT REMOVE
DATE DUE CARD FROM THIS POCKET**

MINNEAPOLIS PUBLIC LIBRARY

The borrower is responsible for all books drawn on his card and for fines on his overdue books. Marking and mutilation of books are prohibited, and are punishable by law.